M000029141

Journeys of Transformation

Tools for the Trip

Shiela Baker, MA

© Copyright 2015 Shiela Baker
All Rights Reserved
Published by Shamanic Institute of the NorthWest
Seattle, Washington

Library of Congress Control Number: 2015910634

Printed in the United States of America

No part of this publication may be reproduced, stored in a retrieval system or transmitted in any form or by any means, electronic, mechanical, photocopying, recording or otherwise, without the written permission of the author.

Although the author and publisher have made every effort to ensure that the information in this book was correct at press time, the author and publisher do not assume and hereby disclaim any liability to any party for any loss, damage, or disruption caused by errors or omissions, whether such errors or omissions result from negligence, accident, or any other cause.

This book is not intended as a substitute for the medical advice of physicians. The reader should regularly consult a physician in matters relating to his/her health and particularly with respect to any symptoms that may require diagnosis or medical attention.

ISBN-13: 978-0692412251
ISBN-10: 0692412255

Cover painting by Willow B. Norris, willownorris@hotmail.com
Editing and cover design by Anita Lorene Smith and Shannon Golden.

Journeys of Transformation

Tools for the Trip

Shiela Baker is a shaman. She stands with a foot in both worlds, able to move back and forth gracefully between this world and the world of Spirit. Indeed, for her these worlds have merged and become one. This mundane world of bills, kids, soccer games, and business is permeated with the Spirit world of totems, rock spirits, play, and ancestor spirits.

Shamanism is an ancient form of being aware in this world. It is pan-cultural and found in some form in almost every religion. Yet it is not a religion itself. Rather it is a set of tools used to interact with the Spirit world. One uses these tools on behalf of the community, in service to others. In doing this service you yourself are healed and joy infuses your life.

It is said, "When you are ready, the teacher will come." But pay attention, because the teacher may be a rock, the call of a bird, a synchronistic meeting with an old friend, or this book and mp3, *Practical Shamanism*, available on www.shielabaker.com. Spirit moves in subtle and strange ways that take the eye of the shaman to see and understand. It is our choice to respond consciously or not. But respond we will, so … pay attention!

Shiela Baker knows about Spirit. She knows it down deep in her bones. This book and mp3 are a distillation of her work with the Spirit world. She has been "there." Now she is offering an ancient road map to all of us, to help us find our "Way."

Richard L. Gossett, Psychotherapist and Cross-cultural shaman

Gratitude

I have great gratitude to my early students who helped me be brave enough to develop my own style of drumming, and encouraged me to move beyond what I had learned. I am grateful for my first spirit guides who demanded that I always do more: study with human teachers yet be willing to trust the guidance of Spirit.

On this plane my sincere gratitude goes to my friend, colleague and editor, Kim Pearson. I am grateful to my friend and colleague James Lowe, who helped me with my mp3s at his place of peace, Blessingstead. James' knowledge of music, grace and ease make recording happen effortlessly. I am grateful to Carl Lopes who played percussion on my mp3 and is a wonderful singer of Native American sacred songs.

Gratitude also goes to my first shamanic teacher, Sheila Belanger. And one who continues to inspire me is the Dalai Lama, who like me believes that "the very purpose of life is to experience happiness." My students know that my credo is "we are here to live in bliss." And profound thanks to Deepak Chopra for saying that out loud and repeatedly.

I acknowledge my parents. One said, "Be different, be unusual, be an independent individual." The other asked, "Why are you always trying to shock people?" This juxtaposition of guidance was challenging as well as freeing. One or the other was sure to be pleased!

Shamanic journeying takes us out of ordinary limited reality and into the realm of infinite possibility. I am grateful for the hundreds of student seekers who have journeyed with me. To those who have shared their journeys – many thanks! You enrich your own lives and the lives of all you touch.

Humble heartfelt gratitude to the ancient ones who were called to be shamans. If you too are called and willing to respond, may blessings be upon you. The journey is long but rewarding.

Aho

Table of Contents

Part Three: Continuing Your Journey   *191*

Why I Wrote This Book

My dream for our planet is that we heal our wounds, find our passions, and share our joy.

Shamanism is my passion and my life's work of service. Through the practice of shamanism I am able to heal my own wounds, and it is my joy to share this process with others. It is through the practice of shamanism and the use of its most powerful tool, the journey, that transformation occurs. It is my hope that this book assists each reader in their own healing and in living their life holy. In this way we will heal the world.

We are living at a crossroads in history. An ancient Hopi story tells us that "we are the ones" – the generation the world has been waiting for. What Jung called the "collective unconscious" has transmuted into the "collective conscious," and we are at the jumping off place into another phase of evolution. We have access to the old teachings and the new ways of communication. We needn't be constrained by dogma, but can draw forth its wisdom. What we do, think, say, and feel – all of us, individually and collectively – can make a great difference. By using shamanic journey practice as a tool of accessing our built-in guidance system, we can ensure that the difference we make brings us closer to Spirit. You do not need to become a shaman in order to practice shamanism, just as you do not have to be a priest in order to practice Catholicism. Shamanism is a path of wisdom that everyone can walk.

Spirit wants us to be happy, fulfilled, and whole. In the journey process we are connected to the deep unconscious and are able to receive guidance from our personal spirit guides and allies. We bring Spirit into matter and matter into Spirit.

Shamanism connects us to Spirit in a practical way that is grounded in the present. Unlike psychotherapy, it does not require that you re-experience your past traumas in order to heal from them. In the journey process you learn how to access your personal guide and how to develop an intimate bond with this being. Your guide is always available. If you awake at two o'clock in the morning bathed in sweat and shaking with anxiety, you don't have to wait until nine o'clock to get help from your therapist, your friend, or your mother. You can journey at any time to ask your guide for wisdom, comfort and support – and you will receive them.

Journeying is a natural healing process. I have interwoven shamanism with other healing modalities such as astrology, earth based spirituality, and psychology into a form I call *Practical Shamanism*. My aim in this book is fourfold: to teach you how to journey; to explain how to interpret the messages you receive; to show how to apply them to your life in everyday reality and to use these journeys as a healing path to wholeness. My mission is to illuminate the path that brings journeys of transformation into your everyday life.

Time has sped up and we are privileged to witness that many more teachers, healers and personal growth programs have emerged. Humankind is evolving rapidly and shamanic journeys are powerful, delightful, whimsical, and deeply personal healing paths for transformation.

When I first began teaching the original thirteen journeys outlined in this book, people stayed in their canoes for all their journeys. Now even in the first journey, students are abandoning the canoe to explore. No longer are they waiting for permission to move beyond what and how I knew and guided then.

Your journeys are like you – unique, individual, rugged, funny, constrained, annoying, perplexing and expansive. Some journeys will give you great insights; others will leave you more confused. Sometimes you can return exactly where you left off and continue on your adventure. Many times, I have returned to a journey to notice that I have returned to the place where I left off in the last journey. The information gathered in these connected journeys then helped my process of healing from trauma. These ongoing journeys helped me become a better teacher. The shaman is the wounded healer. My belief is that we heal our wounds, find our passionate purpose and share our joy and wisdom. We are interconnected to all beings.

The art of journeying is profoundly therapeutic. As a seasoned therapist when I discovered shamanic journeying I was delighted. No longer did I wait for my "50 minute hour" to meet with my therapist or my clients; they and I could journey any time day or night as we were moved to do so.

My spirit guides were available any time for me and the guidance I received was never duplicated in a human being. Shamanic journeys are the perfect place to explore your innermost personal inquiries. Even issues, that after many months or even years you have not disclosed to your therapist or advisor, can be accessible. Some things even after intense therapy are still too painful and deeply traumatic to talk about. These deeply personal issues can be more easily discussed with your trusted spirit guide.

My students have unearthed past hidden trauma and abuse in their lineage. With this knowledge they have affected change in their family dynamics. One student discovered that her mother had been sexually abused as a child. This explained why she was not allowed sleepovers at the grandparents' home. She gently explored this with her mother and a healing was possible. Not everyone will make use of the information in the same way. But spiritual guidance also suggests ways of exploring the knowledge with a compassionate caring approach.

Through the process of shamanic journeying and applying the principles learned in these journeys people are able to trust their spirit guides and gain more confidence. By practicing the wisdom, sometimes in meditation or very practical physical ways, physical symptoms of headache and anxiety have greatly decreased. My students' experiences have brought them more joy, more vitality and ability to relate to the world in playful, expressive, creative ways.

My Moose taught me humility when I complained how cold the water in which we were wading was. After a few minutes of listening, he butted me with his huge head and I landed in the cold Canadian waters. Drenched, I got up sputtering. With disdain he asked, "How much room on the Earth do my feet take up?" I looked down and said, "Maybe a square foot?" He looked at my feet and asked the same question. I replied, "Maybe a square foot?" He asked how much I weighed and I lied.... He asked me to guess how much he weighed. I ventured a guess and he corrected me proudly saying he weighed 850 pounds and that our feet took up pretty much exactly the same amount of space on the planet and that I ought to "Shut up with the whining." I learned not to complain from that interaction. This made my life a lot happier as I now think of Moose feet when I want to make something about my life wrong and therefore complain.

Now people are able to journey anywhere, anytime they chose. Your journeys are unique just like you, never in the past, present or future will there be any two journeys exactly alike. If you do not journey, your journeys will never ever come to pass. And the information will never be expressed. Don't miss this opportunity to grace the Earth with your unique wisdom, humor and tears.

And most of all we will miss your unparalleled voice as a healing of our home and loving Mother Earth. These journeys will fill your own home and life with crystals, stones, statues, laughter and tears, plants and animals to remind you how powerful and profound your journey here on Earth truly is.

Everyone can learn this process. When you walk this path, miracles can and do appear.

Journeys of Transformation is more than teaching about the shamanic journeying process. There are many tools for change, for transformation. Most of us don't think about change as transformation; we focus on change. And then we resist the change. But *transformation* somehow is more sexy, more appealing, so we are more interested in transforming than we are in changing. And yet, the only constant is change!

My goal in writing *Journeys of Transformation* is that you use some of the tools introduced in this book for your personal transformation. Whether it's the journey process, whether it's going on a vision quest, whether it's finding a power animal and working with that power animal, or whether it's opening the Akashic Records you will find that there is your information for you about your process and about your passion and your purpose, and therefore, for a lot of us, our prosperity.

There are many pathways to healing, and no one is better or more right that any other pathway. Sometimes we use a trail to get to a destination. We rest there for a little bit. It's like sitting on a bench overlooking a vista, you've gotten to the top of the mountain, to the top of the hill and you're overlooking. You rest a bit and then you find another pathway down. You don't necessarily take the same route back. The same is true in growth and change. Also you might, while you're sitting in that place overlooking the vista, you might look and go, oh, I can climb higher. You might not have noticed that you were on a climb to get to the vista. You might not even notice there's another hill. So when you're there and you're resting and you're getting accustomed to the new you, the changes that you've made, you start to look around and there's another vista. So that gets you to go back into the process again.

Journeys of Transformation is a manual, if you will, that can be used over and over and over again, giving you new insights. Same guides perhaps, different guides maybe. One of the things that I've noticed over the years is that I don't always have the same guide. My guides that were there early in the journey process are now off on the side somewhere. Occasionally they'll come back, they'll pop in to give me some information or give me some encouragement. My business guide has been the same for years, hasn't changed. It's the Giraffe. And the vista that she sees is very different than the vista that I'm privy to, so she's a wonderful guide for that.

My vision, my goal, my passion is that people find, and this is going to be contrary to what a lot of people believe, but that they find an easy pathway. That in my opinion life isn't meant to be a struggle. You don't have to struggle your way up the mountain. You can take a tried and true path or you can forage around in the underbrush and go that way. And different people are going to have different modalities of getting there, different pathways.

My mission is to go out with my little machete and clear a pathway for you so it doesn't need to be that much of a struggle. Because as you will come to know, I believe were are here to live in bliss, and if somebody has already cleared a path, it's going to be much more blissful. That doesn't mean there's not going to be mosquitoes along the way or that you won't see an occasional bear. But you'll have a pathway that has been utilized by others and you will have a guide. No one goes to Everest without some sherpas. And so here's a way for you to have a pathway and to have someone hold your hand along the pathway. And sometimes the pathway is narrow, so you have to go single file so they'll be in front of you. Sometimes the pathway needs to be cleared, so you want them in front of you. Sometimes you want to see what it looks like, so they'll be behind you, giving you the little push up. And so this desire that I have that everyone have a trusted ally to walk the path with is really what I think is useful for people and why you would want to take this life journey with these tools.

To have guidance is a bit like stumbling around in the dark then somebody all of a sudden hands you a flashlight. Guides are not going to turn all the lights on; there are still things for you to figure out on your own. You still have to find where everything is, but here's a light. You can shine it whichever way you need to shine it. And occasionally that flashlight needs some new batteries. Because the light will sometimes get dim. You don't throw the flashlight away, you don't go back to the start and go, oh the light got dim, so I have to start all over. But you can go out and get recharged. And part of the recharging is going back and doing another journey and asking for more information. Or maybe, learning to open the Akashic Records for yourself or finding someone to do that for you. So you get even more information about not just your pathway, your personality's pathway, but the soul pathway. Because ultimately, we're here to learn soul lessons. That's why they call it Earth School. I love that. I love the analogy of the flashlight. A bonfire isn't going to work because it's stationary. So this is giving you another tool for your spiritual toolbox.

So when you do your journeys and then you learn the Akashic Records, you can use both, so here's a bigger light or here's a second one.

And there are many ways to get divine assistance. Prayer is one. How I see accessing the Akashic Records is praying directly and asking very direct questions. They're not obtuse, and when you ask an obtuse question you get an obtuse answer. For example, I was teaching a class and someone asked where they were to live to fulfill their life purpose. So what they got was a lot of kind of fog. I asked, do you know what your life purpose is? And she said, no. If you don't know your life's purpose but you're asking where to live it's going to be really difficult for Spirit to help you find a home to suit an unknown purpose. Perhaps you need to find your home base and from that home base, discover the purpose. Focus on one question or the other; when you combine them in that particular way and you ask the question, then fog comes and confusion comes.

Having a teacher or mentor to also assist you in the clarification of the questioning is often really useful. I encourage people to not just go it alone, but to form a group, and in their group, share those things. Because all by ourselves, we have only our concept of possibility. But when I share with you the possibility that I want to create, then I've got what you've got going, and if I'm fortunate enough to share with four, six, eight, twenty people, then I have all energy focused on my asking. With the old way, if you wanted something, you didn't speak about it, seems to me morphing into the more people you tell, the more energy goes there, and the more energy that goes, the bigger it gets without you having to do it all alone. Your spiritual allies become really helpful in formulating a plan that you couldn't necessarily have done all by yourself. They might have input that you haven't even considered yet. If you don't speak it then it doesn't have the power to manifest. And that's kind of a new concept in some spiritual realms.

The old ways taught us that you don't speak of your desire, you hold it close to your heart. We are relearning a communal teaching as we've grown and evolved and changed over time since these old spiritual concepts took hold. We are joining resources with one another globally.

We are crafting a brand new way of thinking about connection, and heaven knows that the Internet and Instagram and all of those tools through technology have allowed us to have connections with people all around the planet. You don't even have to be in the same country or the same generation as the people you're journeying with, which is really lovely. Because not only then do you get their input from whatever age they are, but you get that different cultural view as well. Sometimes we have to let go of the old ways, and sometimes that is hard for people, because we were taught a certain thing. Now we're crafting more what's true for us and looking at old teachings and the beliefs around those teachings.

We live from our beliefs. We have no other way to live. We believe that family is a man, a woman, and some children, in this culture. In other cultures, family is grandma and grandpa and aunts and uncles and ... you know, it's the seven generations back and the seven generations forward that constitute family. So we're also getting that lovely culture influence from other traditions and other cultures that says we are no longer limited, we are not small.

This is a conscious conversation between you the reader and the book which speaks to the idea about looking at your life. Learn to release that which is no longer serving and draw in that which will better serve.

How will someone know if these concepts are going to work for them or is right for them? It's a little bit like tasting something brand new. First of all, I say, give it a go. I don't say *try* because *try* allows us to be unsuccessful. And everyone knows that no one tries to pick up their coffee cup in the morning. They pick it up. My encouragement to you is to go on a journey, use the Sacred Drumming mp3, *Practical Shamanism*, available on www.shielabaker.com, ask for a guide, get some friends together and journey together so that you've got some people who know you and who can say, oh, I saw this in your journey. The sharing of it is really important. If you know someone who's teaching journeying in your area, go and learn. If you know someone who's opening the Akashic Records and you're curious about what that's about, then by all means, go and get someone to open the Records for you. The more you experience what's being offered in this book, the more your life will be sunny. The fog will begin to clear, the depression, the status quo will begin to lift, you will start to feel more whole and happy. And I think that's the ultimate goal is that you're more whole, you're more happy, and you're more healthy.

So, experiment with it. Some things will work for you, some things won't. Maybe on a Tuesday it's not a good day for you to journey, but maybe Thursdays are your best day for journeying. Let me share how I used this information before I wrote this book. I found out by going through the process of exploring what sign the moon was in for an entire year, that when the moon was in Aquarius, I couldn't get what I wanted for my clients when I was advocating for them. The Moon goes through the zodiac cycle in twenty-eight days, so it stays two and a half days in each zodiac sign, by tracking that cycle for an entire year I made a discovery! I began to use that information to schedule meetings in times when the moon wasn't in Aquarius.

As you do the process, as you learn more about the journey process, as you learn about your guides, as you begin to connect with your Masters, Teachers, and Loved Ones in the Akashic Records, you'll notice that things get easier because you've learned something and you know when to schedule something, you know when to walk through the doorway and when to just wait. So there's a really important lesson in there – that not every day is a good day to walk through every doorway. In some cultures, they go grocery shopping every day. In our culture, we don't do that. We go when it's timely. There's something really important about learning that about and for yourself. For everything there is a season, and some seasons you're going to be outward – think about summer in your culture. Winter is a time of introspection and hibernation. So you learn really a lot about yourself and how you are in the world.

Aho*

*Aho is a shortened version of a Native American word meaning the interconnectedness of all beings. I use Aho as a blessing, much like "Amen" or "So be it."

My Path into Shamanism

When I was five I was on a dock and bent down to wash my hands and I fell into the water. Now, I might have been down there for just a couple of seconds or it might have been longer, but it left a lasting impression on me. On the drive home, I'm thinking we were at a lake, I was sitting in the back seat. Between my parents, I could see my brother, sitting in the front seat. I thought, "What's up with that?" Because, you know, here I am, all cold and shivery in the back seat, and he's sitting between my parents. *I* should be there! Now, he was not actually born for another three years. I was five when that happened; he was born when I was eight.

When I was about seven, people would ask me for my opinion about things. They would tell me what was going on in their lives and I would offer some suggestions. By age ten, eleven, and twelve, I knew that if people did what I had suggested, things got better. I watched people actually take the advice and use it in their lives, and then things would change. And for some people who didn't follow whatever information came through me, things didn't get better. I understood that getting advice is useful, but you've got to do something with it. So that's how it kind of started.

When I was twelve, my paternal grandmother, who had been really loving and gentle with me, crossed over. After this I felt her presence, kind of like she was sitting on my right shoulder whispering in my ear. I would go to do something, and I could hear her giving me advice like, "Oh, do you really want to go and do that?"

Then by the time I was fourteen and fifteen, I had the idea that I had chosen my parents. Being angry and going through that adolescent rebellion stuff seemed kind of ridiculous to me, because if I had actually chosen these people, why would I want to be antagonistic and do all of that? I had a very different adolescence from most people, knowing that the decisions we make affect our lives, and there's no point in being angry about where you are if you've chosen that. So there was a lot more ease in my life at that point.

When I got out of high school, it appeared that the choices I had were pretty limited. What I really wanted to do is to be a mortician because I thought that the way people expressed grief was kind of sad. You know, either everybody kind of held it in and were all stoic or they sort of fell apart, and the falling apart people really kind of got left all to themselves afterwards. So, I thought it would be a useful thing to change that. And I also saw it as a way of financial freedom, because my vision was that I would be so awesome at getting people to express their grief and love for their departed loved ones that a whole bunch of people would come and then I would open up lots of funeral homes and then I could travel. And then I didn't quite know what I was going to do after that, but that didn't come to pass.

What came to pass was that I went to nursing school. After about six or eight months there, I realized that I was in the wrong place because I'm an empath. There were no words for that back then. That was 1965 to 1968. There was no one doing any teaching about empathic behavior, and what I found was I got the symptoms of the diseases that I was studying as a student nurse. I was also diagnosed with epilepsy and manic depression, both of which seemed really ridiculous to me. But my brain waves are different than other peoples'. I went through that pretty much alone. I stopped taking the medication because I couldn't function, so I had a big struggle when I was in nurses' training. My parents wouldn't allow me to stop nurses' training and go to college or university, and I didn't have the gumption to say, "Well, I'm just going to get a part-time job and an apartment and do it anyway." So I stayed.

It was a hard time and it was a really useful time as well. Part of it was because when I found psychiatry, I was at home. I understood it would be wonderful and useful because I understood how people got depressed. I understood how your attitude affects your life and how trauma can really skew things for you.

What I found when I was doing rounds with one of the doctors who had had a lot of experience with LSD, that his experience made him somehow accessible to the patients. As I was standing there and watching, they would have conversations in which I had no idea what they were talking about. But this doctor's patients got better, their medications got reduced, and they had less recidivism. So they didn't leave the hospital, find that they were re-experiencing their challenges, and come back to a hospital again. There was something really important and profound about that. The doctors who appeared to do the best with their patients, from my perspective, were the ones who could kind of talk in a way that made no sense to me. What I know now is that shamanism is about the absurd. And so their conversations were absurd to me and yet, there was healing in them. This in retrospect was my earliest professional shamanic experience.

A few years after that, I was working in the emergency room of a hospital as part of a crisis team. There was a kid, nineteen or so, who came into the hospital because they said he had a psychotic break. He had left Calgary, Alberta, Canada where I was living and run about fifteen miles out to the nearest town and had dinner with his parents. They knew that something wasn't quite right because he was hyper and agitated and probably a little delusional. When I got to meet him, he told a story of being out in the field and having a conversation with a fox, and he said what the fox had told him. Years later, I reflected that this was, from my perspective once again, probably a shamanic initiation. If anyone had understood that, we might have dealt with his "psychotic break" differently.

I watched this happen to a whole number of young people who had four or five stressors in their lives and who had a break from reality. They then got diagnosed with something and treated as if the diagnosis were true. And what I watched was their vitality drained out of them, and I watched them turn into drones. So they had behavior that was lacking in vitality and energy and life force.

I've always been intrigued by how the mind works and how two people could view exactly the same thing differently. When I'm walking on the beach with a friend and talking, when we return and reflect back on that experience, both of us will have completely different experiences. For instance, I may be wearing gloves and a hat, and my friend has none. So, just the fact that we experience the physical world so radically differently is and was a great curiosity to me.

After nurses' training, I met with a group of friends one night and we decided to have a séance. We were up on the sixth floor of an apartment building, still in Calgary, and all the windows were closed and we had our official candles sitting there. And we said, "If there's an entity in the room, flicker the candles three times to the left." The candles went womp, womp, womp to the left, and so we knew we were on track. And then as we started to ask questions and look around the room, the person sitting directly across from me and I both looked startled because I saw a different face on him and he saw a different face on me. So we were clever enough that we said, "Okay, let's stop now," because we had no idea what we were doing and whether the energy that we were inviting in was beneficial or not.

Later on that evening, we did something that was, back in the day, called automatic writing. You use your non-dominant hand and another person sitting across from you uses their non-dominant hand. You hold a pencil and it just starts to write. We did that, and that evening I was gifted with my very first spiritual guide. And as I spent time in this endeavor – now-a-days it would be called channeling – I found out that his name was Ellendese. He told me where he lived, what they were eating, who was in his family, and he told me about Stonehenge. I'm this little hick kid in Calgary, Alberta, Canada, and I had never heard of Stonehenge. My friends asked, "So, Shiela, what's going on?" I said, "Oh, I don't know, he's telling me about someplace called Stonehenge." They said, "Shiela, there *is* a Stonehenge." So, that was a little spooky! I went to the library and got all these books on Stonehenge and found that what he was telling me was actually in books. What he told me about Stonehenge appeared to be accurate. He also told me about events in my life that later came true.

And then there was a time when I had a lot of elves and fairies around – or at least that's what I imagined they were. I would be cooking and chopping, turn around and the knife would be missing. So then I would say, "Okay, put the knife back." And I would turn around, and the knife would be there. Or my earrings would go missing. I also knew, as I was reading these books, because I'm empathic, which means highly suggestible, that I could do what was told in stories in books. One woman would see a man in flames at the end of her bed and knew that someone had tragically crossed over, so it was her devotion to help that soul move on. Sometimes in these books it involved some very practical things like helping people move funds around and that kind of thing.

So as I recognized that I am empathic and I knew that I could conjure up this man at the end of my bed, it kind of frightened me. At that point I had a small child so I decided that I would forego all of that and kind of slammed the door, put this big metal gate down and locked it – put little bolts about every two inches down and said, "No, I can't do this." There were no teachers back then either, so I couldn't get any real help.

Fast forward about twenty years and I'm talking to a girlfriend. I'm living in Boston at the time, and I had become curious about Wicca, and I had attempted to find witches. But they weren't available to me. I went to Salem; I couldn't even find the shop that the witches have there, so I realized that that wasn't the place. As I got ready to move across country and reunite with my daughter, I set an intention to find some witches to study with, because that was what seemed to me to be the oldest thing that I could fathom that connected us to the Divine. When I came to Seattle, I sought out and found a few groups of Wiccans to study with. I even managed to find some Druids. I spent a year and a day with them. But what became apparent was that that was not really my modality either.

It wasn't until I was studying Astrology, which was one of the tools that I wanted to add to my little spiritual toolbox, that I found

Shamanism. I was studying with Sheila Belanger, and she was teaching us Astrology through a monotonous drumbeat. Amazing things were happening. We were doing shamanic journeys to understand Astrology, which is a really fabulous way to really integrate it into your deep knowing. As time went on, we asked her to teach us. What I realized through those teachings was that I had already been doing shamanic work. I didn't understand there were tools available. I'd actually lived my life divinely guided. When I was told to go and study Dance Movement Therapy, and when I'm told things, I pretty much follow the advice that I'm told. I went back to New England to study Dance Movement Therapy.

So here I am in Seattle, I'm studying Astrology, and Shamanism is a big part of the way that Sheila Belanger understands Astrology. We started to work together, and she took me on my first Vision Quest. At that time I was working for a social agency as a Children and Family Therapist. After my first Vision Quest, I realized that I really couldn't go back to that work. It wasn't fulfilling. When I went to go back, literally, I couldn't stand up. So I started to think about the symbolism of the back and how it's about standing up for yourself, something to lean into, and I realized that the work I was doing there didn't have that kind of support. Three weeks later I left. I had one therapy client when I left and wasn't really sure how I was going to manage in life. But here it is, almost two decades later, I live on a bay and have a beach house.

So that's a story of how I got to be a shaman. Now my devotion is to teach others the shamanic journey process as a way to live life divinely inspired. We are here to live in bliss, heal our wounds, discover our passionate purpose and share our joy. I hope you enjoy the journey process and find deep wisdom in your Spirit Guides.

Aho

Part One

Shamanism Revealed

What Is Shamanism?

Shamanism is an ancient spiritual path and one of the oldest known healing practices. It is not a religion, although it requires a belief in the spiritual realm. The origins of shamanism predate recorded civilization and go back many thousands of years to before the Stone Age. It is the oldest way that humans sought connection with the Creator.

Cycles of Nature

All indigenous people, regardless of cultural differences and customs, share shamanic practices. These are rooted in the natural life cycles of the earth and the movement of the sun, moon, and stars through the sky. Indigenous cultures ritually marked the seasons of life such as birth, puberty, marriage, and death. The deep inner spiritual life was honored as they lived closely with the great archetypes of Earth, Sky, Center, and the four directions. Today shamanism still survives on all inhabited continents in spite of the human failures such as materialism, disrespectful treatment of the Earth, determination to control and contain Nature, and dogmatic religious practices.

The word shaman itself comes from the language of the Tungus people of Russia. According to the *Encyclopaedia Britannica*, its derivation is from the Tunguso-Manchurian word *saman*. Anthropologists researching healing practices the world over have applied the term shaman to many indigenous tribal healers and medicine people.

Energy Connections

The work of a shaman is to help us connect our inner and outer worlds, to heal old wounds, and to bring dreams from the world of Spirit into our lives. The most important characteristic of shamans is that they are masters of the energy moving through the human body, known by various names such as *chi* in China, *kundalini* in India, and *ormana* in Hawaii. Shamans know this energy, seemingly invisible, connects all that exists. They know how to use it. They are masters of altered states of consciousness and travel to other realities while in a state sometimes known as ecstasy, in order to learn and bring back the wisdom they have found.

Shamanism is a path to knowledge, and is gained through life experiences, rituals, ceremonies, prayer, meditation, trials, and tests. Shamanic knowledge helps individuals and communities change and grow, meet challenges and overcome obstacles, and recover peace and wholeness. This knowledge is often passed down through family lineage, just like family recipes. Or it may be acquired from individual practice until it is known from the inside, fully experienced by the apprentice until integrated as part of their nature.

Common Cultural Components

Although shamanic practices differ from culture to culture, there are components of shamanism which can be found in nearly all cultures and eras. These include:

- The journey experience is always spiritual in nature, usually involving ritual and the setting of "sacred space."

- The journeyer visits an alternate reality, often called "non-ordinary" reality.

- The journeyer uses the imagination to enter a lucid dream state, or to achieve an out-of-body experience.

- Entry into the lucid dream state is often facilitated by a repetitive, monotonous sound, such as a drumbeat.

- The outcome of the journey is frequently healing in nature, and always involves change of some kind, either for the journeyer or the community.

While a shaman uses the journey process as a vital tool, not everyone who journeys needs to become a shaman. This requires years of study and practice. The shaman is a visionary, prophet, healer, ceremonialist, and psychotherapist. She or he is the "Doctor of the Soul" for both the community and individuals. The shaman is always concerned with the spiritual health of the people as a whole. She or he keeps the vision alive of who they are and where they are going. The community may become dispirited and it is with the shaman's help that it regains its focus and passion, equilibrium, connection, and balance.

Imagination and Consciousness

The shaman's normal state in the journey is ecstasy. Ecstasy comes from the Greek *ex-stasis*, meaning outside the normal state of consciousness. "Ordinary" people, to quote the Armenian teacher Gurdjieff, live in a state of "waking sleep." The shaman is someone who has woken up to the reality of other worlds. Indeed, the existence of this reality is the basis of shamanism. This reality has been described as the "nagual" or other dimensional reality, the reality behind apparent reality, and the reality of imagination. The dismissive statement, "Oh, it's only imagination," is a gross denial of understanding of how the universe really works. It is in the imagination, the thought or dream realm, where all is first conceived. Our material world, the world of matter, is but a reflection of the dream realm. It is in the journey process that this communication with other realities occurs.

Existing in Both Worlds

To practice shamanism is to stand with one foot planted in the physical world and the other planted in the spirit world – and to exist fully in both at the same time. Shamanism involves fantastic inner journeys into the collective unconscious. Dramatic initiation experiences of shamans often involve death-rebirth sequences, and other powerful or unusual experiences. Shamans have experiential access to other levels and realms of reality and can facilitate non-ordinary states of consciousness in other people for healing and transformation. The shaman is a specialist in spiritual practices and communication with the Spirit world.

The spiritual beliefs of the shaman can be anything from simple animism to a complex system of deities and helpers, and does not exclude traditional Western religious beliefs. Belief is necessary because the shaman is involved deeply in the world of spirit. The shaman may be seen as a Magician with the power to cure, a Poet, a Mystic, or a Priest. She or he has contact with the higher and lower regions and their inhabitants, nature spirits, planetary allies, and a myriad of others. This contact with spirit guides and helpers enables the shaman to affect healing and convey teaching stories from the journeys upon return to material reality.

Shamans journey for other individuals and communities, but you do not have to undergo a lengthy training process to experience the journey process and its healing qualities for yourself. Journey experiences are readily accessible to any student. Once the experience of journeying is learned, you will always have access to your guides.

In the past shamanism was considered the realm of mystics and medicine people only. Some people still believe this, but I do not. In fact, I believe my task in this life is to blow that misconception out of the water. Shamanism is a path for everyone, every culture, every age, every sex. The journey tool can be productively and practically used for guidance on every experience, every fear, every decision, every hope, every desire.

Aho

Other Tools of the Shaman

As you continue to deepen your journey process, there are other shamanic tools available to you, and further studies you can pursue in shamanism. Shamans are healers, teachers, and conduits between non-ordinary reality and the physical world of our five senses. We know there is actually no division between these worlds, and it our mission to enlighten others to this fact.

Shamans use the journey process to heal others – other people, creatures, objects, their communities, the earth, and the universe itself. We journey on behalf of these others, doing the necessary work in non-ordinary reality to heal and make whole those who are broken or wounded.

Like anything else, learning to journey for another being takes training, time and energy. If the work of a shamanic healer is something you are called to do, there is training available in the healing processes such as soul retrieval and soul extraction, from shamans all over the world as well as myself. Similarly, if you feel that you would benefit from shamanic healing processes, there are shamans who can help you by performing soul retrieval or soul extraction.

Although these healing modalities are not the subject of this book (they would fill a book by themselves) here is a brief description of these important shamanic concepts, to help you decide if you would like to walk this path.

For the shaman, all disease – physical, mental, or emotional – is a result of soul loss. I imagine the soul to be like an orange with segments. When traumatic things happen, these segments may split off from the whole and move into the other world. They "pop out" to protect us from pain. There is a broad spectrum of traumatic events that may cause soul loss, including everything from emotional, physical, and sexual abuse, to divorce, to watching one's parents argue, to car accidents, to not being invited to a birthday party when you were five years old. Over time, these events can lead to feelings of "being outside yourself," "disconnected," "living in a dream," or "in pieces." Trauma is not the only way soul loss occurs. You may give part of yourself away to someone you feel deeply about. If someone you love leaves you, even through death, they may take a part of you with them. Or if someone has great power over you, they may "steal" parts of your soul. You experience this as powerlessness.

Many times our lost soul parts spontaneously return to us, but sometimes they get stuck in the other world. This may manifest in the physical world as dis-ease, such as chronic depression, ulcers, heart disease, cancer, asthma, or any other infirmity. Or it may manifest as a series of "bad choices" such as entering into abusive relationships, abusing alcohol or drugs, or other addictive behaviors.

To heal soul loss, the shaman journeys to the Other World/Akashic Records on behalf of the afflicted person. The objective is to restore wholeness. Oftentimes the lost soul part is "held" by guardians in the Other World/Akashic Records, who have been keeping it safe, sometimes for years, and do not want to let go. The shaman, with the help of his or her spirit guides and allies, communicates with these guardians, sometimes praising and cajoling, sometimes bartering, sometimes applying a little force. To be successful in retrieving the soul part, the shaman must have developed strong relationships with powerful spirit allies. Otherwise this process can be quite dangerous to the shaman herself.

Before retrieving the soul part, the shaman is often called upon to perform an extraction. Extraction is necessary when something entered into your body that is no longer serving you. It is often very old. For example, if alligators show up in my journey to retrieve someone's soul part, I know immediately that this person has experienced intense wounding in the past, which is now locked in their body. My alligators always do the deep extraction work, because they are prehistoric, ancient beings intimately knowledgeable about the depths of the past. They are strong, ferocious, and unyielding in their quest.

Extraction work makes space for the soul part to return. The shaman then asks the soul part (or parts) if they are ready to return. If they are not, the shaman continues to do the necessary work to convince the soul part that it is now safe and wanted. When they are ready to come home, the shaman blows them into the client's heart and crown chakra. It is at this point that the client's work begins.

One of the beauties of shamanism is that the shaman actually does all the initial work. The client doesn't have to dredge up old painful memories, reliving and re-experiencing them. This is done by the shaman. The shaman will bring back pieces of information to the client. I often bring back scenes, which I describe to my client. These scenes mean nothing to me, and often make no sense at all. That's okay. It's not my job to make sense of it. The scene may be a metaphor for something, or it may be a past life memory, or it may be part of the client's actual experience. Sometimes the client doesn't recognize the scene either. They may be disappointed at first, saying something like, "But that makes no sense!" It has been my experience, however, that within a short period of time, usually a few days or weeks, they will suddenly "get it" and the scene will make sense to them.

After the soul part is retrieved and returned, the dialog between the soul part and the client begins. The soul part left because its needs were not being met, or it got scared out. It needs reassurance and a commitment from the person that this time it will be taken seriously, and protected from harm. This is a serious endeavor, not to be undertaken lightly. If you are considering having a soul retrieval, remember you are taking on an opportunity to not only heal yourself, but your ancestors and the generations that come after you.

People who have had soul retrievals and followed through on their commitments to the integration work, have been changed dramatically. Yet the effects may seem subtle to others. You are still the same person, but now with a sense of being "all together." You may be asked, "Did you get a haircut?" or "Are you wearing a new outfit?" because people know something is different, they just don't know what. Your natural radiance, once clouded, is now shining.

Aho

What Is a Journey?

Shamanism is simply a means of uncovering and focusing your personal power. The primary tool of shamanism is the journey, the process of consciously moving beyond the physical body into the realm of spirit. This spirit world has been called "non-ordinary reality," the "Other World," "the spirit realm," or the "collective unconscious." It is a real place. Reality exists in the mind.

The Spirit Realm

To enter the spirit realm, we use the technique of the lucid dream state, which simply means that you know you are dreaming. You are deeply relaxed, and are both awake and asleep. You are both the actor and the watcher in the journey. You travel between the worlds of ordinary reality and non-ordinary reality, with a foot in both. Your own imagination is the gateway to this world.

To enter the lucid dream state it is often helpful to concentrate on a monotonous sound, such as a drumbeat. You then "follow the drumbeat" past your own consciousness and enter into the Other World/Akashic Records. Each of us has helping spirits available to us in the spirit realm. During the journey these beings will make themselves known to you. They may have messages for you. They may be there to help you with healing your wounds, or the wounds of others. They may be there to tell you a story. They may simply be there to keep you company.

Trust

Each person's journey is different, and there are no "rules" or "off limits" areas for what constitutes a journey. Some people report that "nothing much happened," and others recount fully realized, plot driven stories. But unless your brain has ceased activity, you are experiencing something. The key to the journey experience is trust. Trust that your guides are there. Trust that this realm does exist. Trust yourself.

Many beginning students are worried that they are "just making it up." My response is always, "Okay." Whether you are consciously "making it up" or unconsciously creating the journey experience, *it does not matter*. The truth and power of the journey experience are the same. Our imagination is the vehicle that brings us into the spirit realm. It is not merely acceptable to use it, it is essential.

Journeys help us to create our own myths. We bring information from the spirit realm into ordinary reality, and build our lives around that information – *as if* it was real. When we do, these two realities begin to vibrate at similar frequencies, until we are actually living our journeys. We turn non-ordinary reality into reality.

Connection with the Universe

The shamanic technique of journeying offers a way to "wake up" your own potential, and explore your spiritual relationship with the universe. Journeying helps you to maintain balance and harmony within yourself, and opens a connection with Mother Earth and All Creation. Our ancestors lived in close relationship with Nature. They knew the ways of animals, they understood plant medicine, and they paid attention to the turning of the Wheel of the Year in the passing and returning of the seasons. Living in an urban environment has taken us far from this shared knowledge. In shamanic journeys we have the ability to reclaim our ancestral heritage, and commune with these carriers of deep knowing.

Shamanic journeys can help all beings enjoy a creative and fruitful life, dance the dance of joy, and become part of the solution of living harmoniously on Earth. We are all here to bring Spirit into matter and matter into Spirit.

Aho

How to Journey

The heart of this book begins with Part Two, where you begin the exciting process of learning how to journey. We walk through each of the fourteen journeys we take together, step by step. The steps are always the same and easy to learn, and when you have learned them you will know how to journey. However, there is no right way or wrong way to journey, just as there are no right or wrong journeys. The processing of journeying leads each of us to our own individual truth.

It is also up to you to decide the frequency of journeying. As you are learning you will be building momentum and a relationship with your guide. This process cannot be rushed or forced. You must follow the timing that is right for you. I recommend that you journey once a week for the first five journeys, and after that as you are called.

Use the following steps as a guide for your learning process. They have been useful for thousands of journey students, and it is my hope that they will be so for you. These steps are briefly repeated in each journey chapter for ease of use.

Step One: Smudge

In my practice, I always smudge before embarking on any spirit work. Smudging is an ancient tradition in many indigenous cultures, used to purify the area and the participants.

Place a slow-burning plant material, such as cedar or sage in a natural holder such as an abalone shell, light the material, and fan the smoke over you and the room with a feather or your hand. It is the symbolism that is important, so if smoke bothers you do not light the plant material. Just pretend to do so.

Step Two: Set sacred space

When you set sacred space you are signaling to the spirits that you are serious about this process and the sacredness of your life. You are asking for Spirit's protection and help in your journey to the spirit realm. Setting sacred space can be done in many ways; it is the intention that is important. In my tradition I "Call in the Directions" and light candles which represent each of the four directions, plus Earth Mother, Sky Father, and Creator. When I journey with others we sit in a circle. The circle symbolizes connection between all beings.

It is not necessary to light the candles each time you journey, but I encourage you to do so because it helps to focus your intent.

You will also find the instructions for Calling in the Directions on the Sacred Drumming mp3, *Practical Shamanism*, available on www.shielabaker.com   Refer to this section at the start of each your journeys. Once you have learned these steps, you will not need to read these directions each time unless you want to.

In the space where you are journeying, place seven candles on the floor or on a table. Place one candle in the East, one in the South, one in the West, and one in the North. Place three candles in the middle, one each for Sky Father, Earth Mother, and Creator.

Light the East candle, and say:

Spirit guides and allies of the East

Where Eagle soars and Owl is able to look into the deep dark woods

The time of dawn and new beginnings

The place of clear visions and objectivity

The element of air and intellect
We ask you to guide us and teach us and show us the way

Aho

Light the South candle, and say:

Spirit guides and allies of the South

The place of trust and innocence and childlike playfulness

The time of summer and the hot noonday sun

Where Coyote frolics and Snake keeps her belly low to the ground

But her senses ever aware

And Grandmother Spider shows us how to weave it all together
from within

We ask for the good medicine of the South

We ask you to guide us and teach us and show us the way

Aho

Light the West candle, and say:

Spirit guides and allies of the West

The place of watery fluidity and all of those creatures that
live there
Known and some still unknown

The place of Great Mystery still on this planet

And Bear medicine that shows how to walk in isolation
And come together at time of desire and co-creation

We ask you to guide us and teach us and show us the way

Aho

Light the North candle, and say:

Spirit guides and allies of the North

The vast expanse of whiteness, the deep look within time

The time of hibernation and introspection and reflection

Where White Buffalo Calf Pipe Woman brought her gifts to
the people

The place of ancestral wisdom, intuition, and deep knowing

We ask you to guide us and teach us and show us the way

Aho

Light the Sky Father candle, and say:

Sky Father

The place of illumination

The sun, the moon
The planetary allies

We give thanks for support from above

Aho

<u>Light the Earth Mother candle, and say:</u>

Earth Mother

Upon whom we walk

The place of the two-legged, the four-legged,

the creepy-crawlers, the swimmers,

The winged ones, the standing people, the trees, and the rock nation

We give thanks for your ability to take that which no longer serves

Compost it and bring it back into sustenance and nurturance

We give thanks for support from below

Aho

<u>Light the Creator or Great Spirit candle, and say:</u>

Creator

The Great Hoop of Life that binds us all

We give thanks for the ability to spiral into source

And bring that which we find there back into illumination

We give thanks for imagination, creation, and manifestation

And most of all we give thanks for being held

Aho

Take a deep breath.

Step Three: Set Your Intention

Each of your journeys will have an intention that will be specific to that particular journey. Your intention is what you wish to learn, or to be shown.

Here I give you suggested intentions for each of our fourteen journeys. In my classes I always suggest that your initial journey, even if you have journeyed before, is to ask for a spirit guide to be with you through this series of journeys. Guides can be with you for years, through one event, or for a specific period. Sometimes guides tell us when they are ready to move on or when we have need for another guide.

Subsequent journeys in this series will be to the Other Worlds/Akashic Records – realms of the four cardinal directions, the realms of the ancestors, the realms of the archetypes, and finally to the Upper Realm, Lower Realm, and Center. In each of these realms you will discover spirit allies, lessons, healing, and other personal connections. By journeying to these destinations, you will begin to learn the "landscape" of non-ordinary reality.

You may set your intention to receive information about literally anything. You can ask for guidance on practical matters, such as your job, or emotional matters such as your relationships, or even as a tool for understanding the past or the future. You can visit other archetypes, or planets, or astrological signs, or mythological or fictional characters. You can journey deep into your own past. In the spirit realm there is no time or space. You are free to go anywhere, anytime, in any way.

When setting your intention, it is well to be specific, as Spirit will take you at your word! The language you use will often affect the particular events of a journey. If you say, "tell me what house to buy," you will get different results than if you say, "show me what

I need to know about buying a house." If you say, "Show me what I need to know about the East," you will receive personalized information about *your* East, what is true and meaningful for you about the East, not necessarily what someone else has decided the East means. This is a more focused intention than "My intention is to visit the East." Experiment to see which phrasing works best for you and your guides. I have found that asking variants of "show me what I need to know" to be the most helpful, and this is what I recommend to my students.

Remember to be respectful, just as you would be to anyone. Do not demand; ask. Remember that your guide and other spirit beings have real emotions – they can be happy or sad, offended or pleased, angry or compassionate. Treat them with courtesy and tact. And don't forget to say thank you!

Step Four: Get Comfortable

Now that you have purified your area and set sacred space, you are ready to begin the journey process. This is your journey, so arrange yourself however you are most comfortable – sitting, lying down, on the floor, or on a sofa or bed. People often become chilled when journeying so you may want to cover yourself with a blanket. You may also want to cover your eyes with something such as a scarf, or shut off extra lighting. Nearby have your journey journal, pen and P›ractical Shamanism mp3 available (go to www.shielabaker.com to get your copy). Take some deep breaths and relax.

Step Five: The Journey

Turn on the Practical Shamanism mp3. Follow the instructions on the mp3. If you do not have this mp3, you may listen to other monotonous sounds such as drums, rattles, or chimes, or simply remain in silence.

Begin the entry into the journey with these words:

> *"Imagine placing yourself in a spirit canoe, and that's a birchbark canoe. On your right-hand side, invite your male ancestors, however they show up: two-legged, four-legged, creepy-crawlers, swimmers, winged ones, the standing people, the trees, the rock nation, or any configuration thereof. On your left-hand side, invite your female ancestors, however they show up. In the stern behind you, place your protection, whatever that is for you. In the bow of your boat, invite your spirit guide. State your intention again. And so it begins."*

I ask you to visualize a canoe because it is a recognizable artifact from nearly every culture – a small, one-person boat. Because I am a resident of the North American continent, I use the birchbark canoe, again because most people can easily visualize one. They are a familiar part of our history and heritage. Because a canoe travels on the water, it may be directed or left to move by itself with the current. I have found it to be a flexible travel medium.

Inviting your ancestors to come with you on your journey gives you support and a vast store of knowledge. In the journey we can tap into the reservoir of ancestral wisdom. Your ancestors, like your spirit guide, can show up as anything: human, animal, mythological, mineral, plant life, planets, or a host of other forms. You may have the same ancestors show up for each journey, or they may change over time, or even from journey to journey. We are complex beings.

Likewise your protection may be anything: shields, clothing, animals, flowers, you name it. You place your protection at your back because it is your most vulnerable part. Your protection gives you a sense of security.

Your guide is in front, to take you in the direction you need to go. With the ancestors on both sides and your protection at your back, you are surrounded on all sides by an energy field of love and support. You are not alone.

After "and so it begins," a monotonous drumbeat will start and last for approximately half an hour. Your consciousness will "ride" the drumming into a lucid dream state. Witness what happens.

During the journey you are both observer and participant. Observe who shows up, what they say and do. Observe your surroundings, and how you feel. Be aware of all your senses – you may smell or taste or feel textures, as well as see images. Some people are visual and will actually "see" images. Others might "hear" voices. And still others might have a "sense" or a "knowing." All of these are correct. Don't worry if you are doing it "right." There is no right or wrong in these realms. Trust yourself! If you think that perhaps you are "making it up" or imagining it, be encouraged. Imagination is the gateway to the soul and how we connect with divinity.

Some journeyers become so relaxed they fall asleep during the journey. Some even snore! It is easy to drift in and out of ordinary consciousness. If this happens to you, don't worry. You are still journeying and experiencing non-ordinary reality even if you don't remember it.

Step Six: Record Your Journey

Once you have completed your journey, either by hearing the final drumbeats or by coming to a natural ending, take a few minutes to write down all that you have experienced. The act of writing concretizes the visions. It may also be helpful, as time passes, to look back through your writings at your growth and at any changes that may have occurred. Sometimes the messages from the journeys do not become apparent to us until after years have passed. Often as we write we remember greater detail. As we speak and write our journeys, so they become our lives.

Step Seven: Give Thanks

Practice gratitude! When we allow ourselves to experience thankfulness, we participate in the grace of life.

Extinguish each candle, while saying:

Spirit guides and allies of all the directions,

For the objectivity of the winged ones in the East,

We give thanks for your predatory ability and tenacity,

To see clearly what you want and go after it,

Even though only one time in ten are you successful.

And from the South, we give thanks for Snake who

Teaches us to shed our old skins,

For Coyote who teaches us to laugh at ourselves first,

And Grandmother Spider who shows us how to weave it

all together.

And for the watery fluidity of the West, where we learn

To bring things from the unconscious into consciousness.

And from the North, the deep knowing that many have walked

this path before us.

We give thanks for illumination from above

And sustenance from below

And for the Great Hoop of Life that binds us all.

We ask that any energy that was raised here today

that is not needed on this land

Be carried on the four winds for the highest and best or better

Of those who need it.

Aho

What Do Journeys Mean?

Journeys help us answer four important and powerful questions:

Who am I?

Where did I come from?

What is important to me?

What is the purpose of my life?

Sharing Journeys

We don't answer these questions alone. By sharing our journeys with each other, we are able to partake of others' perceptions and insights, deepening and enhancing our journey experience. By witnessing another's journey, we learn about ourselves. There are no coincidences. If you are witnessing another's journey, you can be sure that somewhere in that journey will be a message for you too.

Interpreting Journeys

Journeys are often used to answer questions. In many indigenous cultures shamans would journey to ask directions on the movement of the tribe, ask for instructions for vision quests, ask how and when to plant crops, and for other practical reasons. It was the shaman's job to ask the questions and receive the answers, for the language of the spirit realm is rich in metaphor and imagery. These metaphors, symbols, and images require interpretation.

Everything in every journey has a meaning and can be considered a message to you direct from Spirit. However, it is important to understand that nothing means anything until we give it a meaning. Meaning comes from within us.

There are many possible ways to interpret the symbols and metaphors present in journeys. My interpretation may differ from yours. There is no "right" or "only" way. Some symbols are universal, some cultural, some deeply personal to the individual. Some "universal" meanings may resonate within you, some may not.

For instance, suppose an oak tree shows up in your journey. You can be sure that oak tree has meaning for you. It's not there by accident. It is up to you to discover what that meaning is. You may do some research into oak trees, and discover that they are rich in universal and cultural symbolism, often associated with strength and longevity in many myths and historical sagas. You could also have a personal connection with oak trees – perhaps your childhood home had an oak tree in the backyard. Perhaps you had a treehouse in an oak tree. In that case, oak trees may symbolize fun, adventure, or safety. Or any combination thereof.

Another good way to understand the symbolism of the oak would be to ask other people what they know about oak trees. This is another benefit to sharing your journeys. We are often wearing our own personal blinders, which prevent us from seeing what is plainly visible to others.

Ultimately, it is up to you to interpret Spirit's guidance, but I have found it most helpful to use an interpretation method based on five archetypes, which is flexible, nonjudgmental, and capable of eliciting profound meaning. It is also easy to learn.

An archetype is a symbolic representation of an energetic presence. Archetypes are symbols which appear in myths in all ages and cultures, but manifest in different ways depending on the individual and their culture. Archetypes are not only found in myths, but also religion, history, and literature. It is easiest to understand them with the help of examples. Some familiar to you might be the "Maiden" archetype, or the "Mother," the "Savior," the "Hero," the "Outcast," just to mention a few. If a woman is planning to do something which requires ferocious courage, for example, she might want to call on the archetype of Kali, a Hindu goddess who is a symbol of feminine power. Visualizing Kali may give her access to the "Kali energy" within her.

In my work, I use five primary archetypes to help us interpret the meanings of our journeys. These archetypes are: the Visionary, the Enlightened Spiritual Warrior, the Teacher, the Healer, and the Magician.

The Five Archetypes

The Visionary is the person journeying because it is you who is going on a journey, a quest if you will.

The Enlightened Spiritual Warrior is an important part of any journey and of your life. Without the Warrior archetype we may all be couch potatoes. The Warrior has get up and go energy. And yet has the wisdom to know when it is wise to wait and be still. When we add enlightenment and spirituality to the Warrior we have raw, available power to align divine intention with action.

The Teacher is the one who understands that every experience has the potential for learning. And that the trick is to implement that which was learned. In ancient times the Teacher was the storyteller, the one who kept the history, the morals and the ethics of the tribe.

The Healer makes us whole. They are the gatekeepers between life and death. All cultures have healers and while each experience has a lesson if we are willing we may also be healed of past trauma, old wounds and deep grief and guilt. This archetype longs for being perfect in every moment.

The Magician is the one who takes a "matter" to Spirit and brings Spirit back into "matter". This archetype makes sure we recall the information we have gathered by making it practical and useful in the physical world. As above so below, when we journey with intention then we affect our everyday world in seemingly magical, unusual ways.

Witnessing Journeys

In my classes, we come together in a circle after journeying to share, witness, and interpret our journeys together. Each person recounts their journey. When they do, they are embodying the archetype of the Visionary. The other class members listen from the perspective of one of the other four archetypes. Then each listener shares the wisdom or messages they heard from that perspective. This process leads to profound insights.

The role of the **Visionary** is to pay attention to the experience he or she is having. An example of the Visionary archetype could be an astronaut on an exploratory mission to a far-off planet. The astronaut's role is to pay attention to what is there, and bring back the knowledge he or she has gleaned. The Visionary watches what is happening without trying to control it. For instance, if you are approaching a waterfall, your mind may anticipate careening down the waterfall. However, in the spirit realm you are just as apt to float off into the air. You are creating your journey, so you can make yourself go down the waterfall, but you could also let go and let whatever happens, happen.

The second role of the **Visionary** is to tell his or her journey as a story – just tell what happened, without blame, judgment, or interpretation. When you are the Visionary, be as specific as possible. Give sensory details. Did you notice a smell, or a sound? What colors did you see? What were you thinking and feeling? Tell all the truth you can remember.

When witnessing another's journey, listen from the perspectives of the archetypes of the **Warrior**, the **Teacher**, the **Healer**, or the **Magician**. Although these perspectives sometimes overlap, each is a distinct archetype that will allow you to understand journeys on a deeper level. Each archetype is *always* represented in *every* journey. Your job as witness is to find them and bring them to consciousness so their wisdom can be known.

The role of the **Warrior** is to "show up" or be fully present in the moment. This archetype is much misunderstood. It does not mean to be cruel, to kill, or to maim. It does not embody destructive energy. A Warrior does not have to go to war. A spiritual Warrior's quest is to be in right alignment with intention. It means always doing your best to the limit of your ability. It means to be vigilant. It means to protect the right. It means to be courageous. When you are listening to another's journey, look for where that person showed these qualities. Where did they show up fully in the moment? When were they brave? When sharing what you found, say, "I saw you show up when you...." or "The Warrior showed up in your journey when you...."

The role of the **Teacher** is to be objective and open to many outcomes, but not attached to them. Objectivity and non-attachment are the hallmarks of wisdom. When you are listening from the perspective of the Teacher, look for a teaching in the journey. Where is there a lesson for the journeyer, or for you? Many times we don't know what we have learned until someone else points it out.

The role of the **Healer** is to be in right alignment with heart. The Healer pays attention to that which maintains the health, joy, and well-being of ourselves and our planet. The Healer facilitates understanding and forgiveness. When you are listening from the perspective of the Healer, look for a healing in the journey. Was there someone or something in the journey who was healed of pain, spiritual dis-ease, or misunderstanding?

The role of the **Magician** is to show us that what you focus on manifests in your life. The Magician takes the Warrior, Teacher, and Healer insights from non-ordinary reality, and brings them into ordinary reality by action. This is the alchemical process of bringing spirit into matter. When you are listening from the perspective of the Magician, look for actions that may be taken as a result of the journey.

From the **Magician** you might suggest that the journeyer find something in ordinary reality that symbolizes their journey. For instance, if the journey had a frog in it, they might purchase a figurine of a frog and place it on their desk or altar. Photographs, paintings, greeting cards, and other illustrations can also serve as reminders of journeys, as well as found objects such as feathers, beads, or rocks. Finding such a representation brings the messages of that particular journey into conscious reality, furthering the connection between spirit and matter. Every time you look at that representation, you are reconnecting with non-ordinary reality and letting it resonate deeper within your body.

Another way to access the **Magician** is to ask the journeyer (or oneself, if you are interpreting your own journey) soul searching questions suggested by the journey. For instance, if you are wearing a veil, you might ask yourself, "Where am I hiding in my life?" or "Am I avoiding facing something?"

Finally, journeys often contain practical guidance for ordinary reality. For example, if the journey contains uncomfortable shoes that hurt your feet, a suggestion from the Magician may be to buy some new, comfortable shoes, or to have a pedicure. Often mundane actions have consequences that are anything but.

Interpreting from the **Magician** archetype brings the divine spark into your daily life. You are bringing spiritual inspiration into consciousness, and then manifesting it on the physical plane. That is the business of a spiritual being having a physical experience.

The insights from archetypes and symbolism can infuse your journeys with added depth, richness, and meaning. Just as with anything else, the more you practice interpreting yours and others' journeys, the more comfortable you will become with the process, and the more wisdom you will be able to glean. Through practice you will find what works for you to bring you closer to Spirit.

Part Two

Journeying Together

Journey to Ask for a Spirit Guide

If you were to go on a trek into a wild unknown country, would you go alone?

Probably not. You would likely seek out someone who had been there before; someone who knew the terrain and could show you how to get to your destination – and how to get back. This is exactly why you need a guide for the journey process. You will be visiting a reality where not only the landscape is unknown, but the rules governing reality are different. Spirit guides know this Other World/Akashic Records as surely as a Sherpa knows the Himalayas. They are here to help, support, and sometimes comfort you. Spirit guides may come to you for a variety of reasons. They may stay with you for a lifetime or come only for certain tasks or to give you answers to specific questions. You may ask for a guide to help you find your life's calling, your life's mate, or even your next house. In this, our initial journey, it will be our intention to find a spirit guide for this series of journeys.

A spirit guide is sometimes called a "power animal," but guides are not limited to animals. Your guide may be an animal, bird, insect, fish, plant, human, mineral, mystical creature, or anything else. There are some shamanic traditions that claim that guides are always animals, and if this is a belief that resonates with you, that is fine. However, I believe in being open to all possibilities, because when we limit possibilities we limit experience as well. My students' guides have included a teardrop, a planet, a bone, a swirling ball of energy, and an automobile, to name a few.

However, it is true that many people find animal guides. Our connection with the other creatures of the earth is far-reaching and profound. We see animals as being close to nature, and thus to Spirit. They do not operate on human agendas and are not motivated by human emotions such as greed or cruelty, which enables us to trust them. Different cultures have close associations with different animals, and animals are associated with many different qualities such as strength, courage, cunning, family connection, and so on. For instance, many cultures and individuals equate the eagle with freedom, so when an eagle shows up in a journey, the concept of freedom may be pertinent for you. Individually, we each have animals with whom we feel connected, a pet or a familiar, or merely an animal you notice continually around you. For example, if wherever you go you notice the presence of crows, you may deduce that the crow has a message for you. (Crows are associated with planning and determination, working in groups, and sometimes trickery. An examination of these concepts in relation to your life would be a helpful exercise.) Animals have much to teach us.

Many of us desire to have a particular animal or creature as our guide. This is our ego declaring its importance. If a squirrel or a canary or a tadpole keeps showing up in your journey, your ego may say, "No, I should have a bear or an eagle or a dragon – something noble and strong!" Or a creature may come to you who you find distasteful or scary. If a guide comes that you feel some aversion for, I ask that you respectfully say, "Thank you, but I'm not interested in having you as my guide." Thanking the creature appeases them and they will often help you find another guide. For example, if in "real" life you have a fear of toads, and in your journey one appears, then thank the toad and ask that he help you find an animal with whom you can form a relationship. This relationship is going to be intimate and assist you with questions about your life, so compatibility is important, especially when learning how to journey. Your aversion to a particular creature may inhibit your ability to learn and enjoy the process of journeying. You will often find that the "unwanted" creature will show up in another journey later on, when you are more comfortable and knowledgeable about the process.

When seeking a spirit guide, it is important to allow it to come to us. I have found that it works better to let Spirit send you a guide, instead of trying to direct Spirit. Some traditions recommend that another person "give" you your guide, or that you consciously choose one yourself. While that technique can be highly satisfying, I have found that an openness to whomever shows up in the journey is a lesson in itself. It is a lesson of surrender and trust, and it often leads you to magical places that you would never have thought of yourself.

In your first journey to request a spirit guide, I ask that you perceive the same creature at least three times, and then ask it if it is your guide. The reason for this is so your ego will get out of the way. The first time you meet the creature your ego may throw up objections or comments, but if you see the creature again and again, the ego will get bored and relinquish control. Then you will be able to accept what your guide has to tell you. You may ask your guide if it has a message for you.

Let us go on our first journey together. Follow these steps, and remember in the spirit realm there is no right or wrong. This is *your* journey.

Aho

Journey to Ask for a Spirit Guide

Here is a brief recap of the steps into your journey. A complete explanation of these steps is found in Part One, *How to Journey.*

Step One: Smudge

Place a slow-burning plant material such as cedar or sage in a natural holder such as an abalone shell. Light the material and fan the smoke over you and the room with a feather or your hand. It is the symbolism that is important, so if smoke bothers you do not light the plant material, just pretend to do so.

Step Two: Set Sacred Space

In the space where you are journeying, place seven candles on the floor or on a table. Place one candle in the East, one in the South, one in the West, and one in the North. Place three candles in the middle, one each for Sky Father, Earth Mother, and Creator. Call in the directions as they are outlined in Part One, *How to Journey.*

Take a deep breath.

Step Three: Set Your Intention

Set your intention to ask for a spirit guide. Say, either aloud or to yourself: "My intention for this journey is to ask for a spirit guide to teach me about the journey process."

Step Four: Get Comfortable

Arrange yourself comfortably, either lying or sitting. Nearby have your journey journal, pen and Practical Shamanism mp3 available (go to www.shielabaker.com to get your copy). Cover yourself with a blanket if you wish. Cover your eyes with a scarf, and dim the lights.

Step Five: The Journey

Turn on the Practical Shamanism mp3. Follow the instructions on the mp3. If you do not have this mp3, you may listen to other monotonous sounds such as drums, rattles, or chimes, or simply remain in silence. Then imagine placing yourself in a spirit canoe, and that's a birchbark canoe. On your right-hand side, invite your male ancestors, however they show up: two-legged, four-legged, creepy-crawlers, swimmers, winged ones, the standing people, the trees, the rock nation, or any configuration thereof. On your left-hand side, invite your female ancestors, however they show up. In the stern behind you, place your protection, whatever that is for you. In the bow of your boat, imagine an empty space where your spirit guide will sit. State your intention again. And so it begins. Witness what happens.

Step Six: Record Your Journey

Once you have completed your journey, take a few minutes to write down all that you have experienced. Be as specific as possible. Remember your senses – what did it look like, smell like, sound like, feel like, taste like? Don't worry about punctuation, spelling, or grammar. Don't be judgmental about yourself, your writing ability, or the "quality" of your journey. This is not great literature. You don't need to write the next great novel. Simply tell the story.

Step Seven: Give Thanks

Many beings have made themselves available to you in the journey. Your ancestors, your protection, the guides and others have showed up for you. It is always nice to be appreciated, as you know. Beings in non-ordinary reality also like to be thanked. Appreciating what you have been given is always good manners. Give thanks as it is outlined in Part One, *How to Journey*.

Sharing and Witnessing the Journey

Remember that when you share your journey with others, and witness their journeys in return, it deepens everyone's experience and increases your understanding of the messages you have all received. It is for this reason that I share my own journeys with you in this book, as well as my interpretations of them. If you are reading this, my journeys will have meaning for you. They have become your journeys as well as mine.

Shiela's Journey to Ask for a Spirit Guide

I notice that I am standing in my canoe. I invite my male ancestors to join me. A large brown bear shows up on my right. I look to the left and invite my female ancestors, and become aware of a Native American elder woman. In my mind I call her the Grandmother.

The bow of the canoe is empty to receive the guide. Behind me I place my protection: a large quartz crystal and two smaller amethyst crystals. The canoe clears the shore and travels along the smoothly flowing river. Without paddling we are carried with the current.

The river bends and before us is a large meadow. The canoe stops at the edge of the water and I get out. I notice that my garments change. I am wearing a medieval apricot-colored costume with flowing skirts and a tall pointed hat with a veil. I have tight shoes with front laces and pointed toes. My feet hurt so I sit on a bench by the edge of a small pond. There are woods around me. I remove my shoes and rub my sore feet.

Out of the corner of my eye I notice movement near one of the trees. I turn my head to see what it is, but just as I do the creature ducks behind the tree. Although neither of my ancestors is with me, I gather up my skirts to venture further into the woods alone. I approach the tree where I saw the movement, and I see another flickering movement further on, near another tree. But before I can identify what it is, the creature again hides behind the tree.

This game of hide-and-seek continues as I go deeper into the woods. I hear a strange sound that seems familiar, although I cannot quite identify it. I look toward the sound and again the creature pulls its head behind a tree. But I have caught a glimpse, and it is now clear that the creature is a bird with a large and showy tail. The bird continues to make its unusual cry while darting behind trees. The cries sound like laughter. I feel as if I am being mocked.

Then I begin to laugh myself. As I do, the bird emerges fully and I see that he is a peacock. I know that he is my guide. I ask if there is a message for me. As if in answer, the peacock flourishes his tail, strutting. Clearly a male bird!

The peacock leads me back to the bench where he rubs my weary feet. He then jumps up onto the bench beside me. As the drumbeat softens he lets me know that we will have other times to talk in later journeys, and he wanders back into the woods. I thank my ancestors and my guide for this experience. The journey has come to an end.

Aho

Interpreting the Journey

Here are some interpretations of my journey. Remember, these are *my* interpretations, and you may agree or disagree with them. You may find meanings in the journey that I do not even mention here. That is wonderful! Each journey contains many layers, many textures, and many meanings.

From the Warrior, who shows up and is ready for action:

I show up when I notice a movement out of the corner of my eye. A function of the Warrior is to scan the surroundings, always ready to be called to action.

I show up when I get out of the canoe without being told. I am showing the ability to decide which appropriate action to take.

I show up when I go into the woods, alone. I am willing to do whatever it takes to find my guide. And even though the guide keeps hiding himself from me, I keep pursuing. I don't give up.

I show up when I do not paddle the boat but allow myself to flow with the current. There are times when the Warrior needs to sit back and observe what is happening, so they can be ready for action at any moment. They do not have to be running around doing things all the time; they must be steady in their observation and willing to let things take their natural course.

- Where did you notice me "show up" in my journey?

Write your thoughts and observations in your journey notebook. You will begin to hone your interpretation skills the more you do this.

From the Teacher, who knows that every journey has a lesson:

I am taught the value of persistence. I do not give up trying to find my guide, even when he tries repeatedly to hide himself. My persistence pays off when he decides to show himself fully.

I am taught about suitability. I get out of the canoe because it is not the correct tool for the moment. If something is not working for us, we can exchange it for a more appropriate tool. Likewise, my attire – the pointy hat and veil, the long skirts, and especially my shoes – is not appropriate for the terrain. I am more comfortable when I remove my unsuitable shoes.

I am taught to lighten up, and not take myself too seriously. It is not until I join the peacock in laughter that he shows himself fully. Things are often not revealed until there is lightness. The peacock teaches me to have fun.

I am taught patience. Although naturally curious to see my guide, I must wait and play the peacock's game before I can see him. By playing hide-and-seek he is counseling me to wait, for all will be revealed in its right time. At the end of the journey he tells me that there will be other times to talk. I don't have to know everything right now.

- Where did you see a lesson in my journey?

From the Healer, who recognizes that each journey has healing potential:

I am healed when I care for my sore feet. We can heal ourselves by treating ourselves gently, and knowing when we need care.

I am healed when the peacock cares lovingly for my feet. I am willing to allow another being to care for me and bring me comfort. This is the beginning of a trusting relationship with my new guide.

I am healed by being willing to receive the foot rub from an unusual source. Who would expect a peacock to rub one's feet? But just because someone doesn't look like they could help you, doesn't mean they can't. Sometimes love comes from unexpected places.

I am healed when I laugh with the peacock. There are few things that offer quicker healing than laughter. It cleanses the heart and soul and allows us to start pure.

- Where did you notice a healing in my journey?

From the Magician, who translates insight into application:

One action might be to obtain a peacock feather, or feathers, and display them in a vase on my table, or arrange them in a pleasing pattern on a wall. I can remain alert for things showing up in my "ordinary" life that remind me of this journey. For instance, a few weeks after I took this journey, I was in a grocery store when I passed by the greeting card rack and noticed a card showing a reproduction of an old painting. The painting was of a medieval woman dressed in an apricot dress and a veil, and holding a peacock. Of course I had to buy the card! I also had it framed and hung it on my office wall. Now every time I see it I am reminded of this journey and the wisdom it had for me.

Another action would be to ask myself some soul searching questions. There is much hide-and-seek in this journey. Am I hiding something from myself? The uncomfortable shoes are a feature of the journey – am I hobbling myself by acting, speaking, or dressing inappropriately? In this journey the peacock did not show himself until I laughed with him. What am I missing when I take myself too seriously? There are many other questions I could explore.

Finally, I could take some practical actions. Perhaps I should buy a new pair of comfortable shoes. Or perhaps I could pamper my feet by treating myself to a pedicure.

- Where did you see an action that might be taken from the insights in this journey?

Some symbols and metaphors present in my journey:

My male ancestor the bear is a universal symbol of physical strength. When bears are provoked they are fearsome. Because they hibernate, they are a universal symbol of introspection, or going within. They are also known as highly nurturing mothers. In European cultures, the bear was sacred to the Goddess Diana/Artemis. Priestesses of her cult often danced in bear guises. Many Native American cultures view the bear as a powerful visionary able to communicate directly with Spirit. Bears also have a personal meaning to me. I was raised near the backcountry woods of Alberta, Canada, and one of our family activities in the early spring was to pile in our truck and go watch the bears foraging at the public dump. Therefore to me the bear signifies a strong connection to my childhood and family.

My female ancestor, the Native American Grandmother, is a powerful symbol. The Grandmother archetype signifies the deep wisdom of the feminine in virtually all cultures. Native American figures and symbols are quite common to people journeying on the North American continent, regardless of their racial heritage.

(Although many North and South Americans, after hundreds of years of intermingling, have Native American blood.) I believe that Native Americans, as the indigenous people of this continent, symbolize the connection to this land and personify the wisdom of the earth.

There are many symbolic meanings for the crystals that are my protection. The quartz crystal is a record keeper. Quartz is used in timekeeping pieces like clocks and watches. It holds onto the old stories. Amethysts connect you to your higher self, and represent the seventh chakra. The universal meaning of crystals is that they refract light. They change and break it into rainbows. They are a symbol of shape shifting. Shape shifting refers to the ability we have in the Other World/Akashic Records to transform into our guides, perhaps we look to our fingers and see talons, claws or feathers. This feat is common in the shamanic realm and allows us to sense and feel as if we are that animal.

My medieval finery may be a symbol for nobility or royalty, since only rich and powerful court ladies dressed this way in the Middle Ages. It symbolizes the age of chivalry, knights in shining armor, slaying dragons, jousting, and a host of legends and stories that to our modern eyes spell "Romance." The veil I am wearing may be another symbol, perhaps meaning that I am trying to hide from something. Or I may ask myself what I am doing to keep myself from being seen?

Tending to another's feet is a metaphor signifying the utmost humility and willingness to serve. Mary Magdalene washed the feet of Christ in homage, and Christ himself taught a powerful lesson in humility when he was willing to wash the feet of his followers.

Finally, there are legions of myths and stories surrounding the peacock. Peacocks have been associated with royalty in Europe, the Middle East, and China, and divinity in India. This ties in with the medieval garb I am wearing, so the royal symbolism in this journey is something I might pay attention to. Am I acting as a queen should? Am I demanding my just due?

The eyes of peacock feathers are symbolic of watchfulness, and are associated with clear vision and wisdom. In Islamic folklore, peacocks are often shown as guards, since their eyes never shut. Many other cultures hold the peacock as a symbol of the "all seeing" eye.

The peacock is associated with vanity and arrogance in many cultures, because of the male's flamboyant, beautiful tail and his fondness for displaying it. However, the peacock is also known for its harsh voice and ugly feet. According to a Hindu tale, the peacock's feet were so ugly that he screamed every time he saw them.

- What symbols did you see in my journey? What universal, cultural, or personal meanings do they have for you?

Interpret Your Own Journey

Now it's your turn to interpret your own journey to find a spirit guide. Reread the notes you took after your journey. Ask yourself questions from each perspective. If you can, share your journey with others. Let them give you their interpretations. Listen.

- From the Warrior, who shows up and is ready for action – where did you show up in your journey? What actions did you take?

- From the Teacher, who knows that every story has a lesson and seeks to find it in the journey – where did you notice a lesson in your journey?

- From the Healer, who recognizes that every event has a potential for healing – where did you notice a healing in your journey?

• From the Magician, who translates spiritual insight into practical applications – what is a "real life" application of the insights you received in your journey?

• What are the symbols you noticed in your journey? What universal, cultural, or personal meanings do they have for you?

Aho

Journey to the East

The next four journeys will take us to the four directions, starting in the East. This allows you to "map" the landscape of your inner reality. I liken this to the floor plan of your house. You know the function and attributes of your kitchen, living room, bedroom, and so on. You know what's there. When you are hungry, you go to the kitchen. When you are tired, you head for your bedroom. It is the same with sacred space. Each direction has different functions, attributes, residents, and meanings. Some are individual to you, and others are cultural or universal.

During these journeys, you will be defining your personal landscape. It is important that you discover your own, and not merely adopt the meanings I may have for any particular destination.

However, there is much information and many universal symbolic meanings about the East, which you may find within your journeys – or you may not. I mention some of these here because you may find it interesting to see where you resonate with your culture, and where you do not. That in itself is instructive.

The East has different meanings in different cultures. These meanings may be mythological, symbolic, historic, literary, or all of these. For many, the East may invoke a vision of the rising sun. For others of a more literal bent, the East might mean the Orient, or even the eastern seaboard of the United States. All of these meanings are correct.

We start our journeys to the directions in the East because when setting sacred space we follow the direction of the sun. The sun rises in the East, so the East is associated with dawn and new beginnings. A fresh new start is possible with each new sunrise. Just before dawn the air is calm and quiet, but as the sun comes up over the horizon, you begin to see and feel the wind through the trees. The clouds gather, scatter, and shift. The East brings about change. When you journey to the East, you may be given messages about new opportunities or changes coming.

The season of the year related to the East is spring, the time of new growth and birth. Spring is when we plant our new crops, our new intentions, and our new hopes. When you journey to the East, you may notice symbols of springtime, such as robins or flowers.

The East is associated with the element of air. Think of the wind. It buffets you around, and can knock you off center, just like a new beginning can. The wind is the breath of life; it's what you take into your body every time you breathe. We are always surrounded by air, even though we cannot see it, only feel its effects. When you journey to the East, you may find whirlwinds, tornados, or tumbleweeds. You may gasp and huff and puff. (Or you may not!)

The East motivates us to look upward, toward the sky, the home of air. Often in journeys to the East, people go *up* – they climb mountains, fly airplanes, ride on clouds, visit planets.

The East rules the mind, knowledge, abstract thinking, and the intellect. The East is often where ideas are generated. You may notice yourself *thinking* a lot during journeys to the East. You may try to "figure it out."

Animals most often associated with the East are the winged ones: birds, bats, dragonflies, or any creatures whose realm is the air. Many people meet birds when journeying to the East. However, this does not always happen, and some people meet land or water animals. If you meet a pig, for instance, that's fine. Maybe it's a smart pig, one who thinks a lot. Also be aware that just because you find chickens in the East, doesn't mean that all chickens live only there.

Other associations with the east include the astrological signs of Gemini, Libra, and Aquarius; the suit of Swords in the Tarot; the New Moon; and the color yellow.

Let us journey to the East to see what the East holds for you.

Aho

Journey to the East

Here is a brief recap of the steps into your journey. A complete explanation of these steps is found in Part One, *How to Journey.*

Step One: Smudge

Place a slow-burning plant material such as cedar or sage in a natural holder such as an abalone shell. Light the material and fan the smoke over you and the room with a feather or your hand. It is the symbolism that is important, so if smoke bothers you do not light the plant material, just pretend to do so.

Step Two: Set Sacred Space

In the space where you are journeying, place seven candles on the floor or on a table. Place one candle in the East, one in the South, one in the West, and one in the North. Place three candles in the middle, one each for Sky Father, Earth Mother, and Creator. Call in the directions as they are outlined in Part One, *How to Journey.*

Take a deep breath.

Step Three: Set Your Intention

Set your intention to visit the East. Say, either aloud or to yourself: "Show me what I need to know about the East."

Step Four: Get Comfortable

Arrange yourself comfortably, either lying or sitting. Nearby have your journey journal, pen and Practical Shamanism mp3 available (go to www.shielabaker.com to get your copy). Cover yourself with a blanket if you wish. Cover your eyes with a scarf, and dim the lights.

Step Five: The Journey

Turn on the Practical Shamanism mp3. Follow the instructions on the mp3. If you do not have this mp3, you may listen to other monotonous sounds such as drums, rattles, or chimes, or simply remain in silence. Then imagine placing yourself in a spirit canoe, and that's a birchbark canoe. On your right-hand side, invite your male ancestors, however they show up: two-legged, four-legged, creepy-crawlers, swimmers, winged ones, the standing people, the trees, the rock nation, or any configuration thereof. On your left-hand side, invite your female ancestors, however they show up. In the stern behind you, place your protection, whatever that is for you. In the bow of your boat, invite your spirit guide. State your intention again. And so it begins. Witness what happens.

Step Six: Record Your Journey

Once you have completed your journey, take a few minutes to write down all that you have experienced. Be as specific as possible. Remember your senses – what did it look like, smell like, sound like, feel like, taste like? Don't worry about punctuation, spelling, or grammar. Don't be judgmental about yourself, your writing ability, or the "quality" of your journey. This is not great literature. You don't need to write the next great novel. Simply tell the story.

Step Seven: Give Thanks

Give thanks as it is outlined in Part One, *How to Journey*.

Sharing and Witnessing the Journey

Remember it is a powerful thing to share your journeys with others, and to witness theirs in return. Here is my journey to the East. It has become your journey as well as mine.

Shiela's Journey to the East

I observe myself sitting in the canoe. Bear is floating in the water on my right. On the left is Grandmother with a group of five young girls gathered around her. In the bow Peacock is preening, and behind me is the crystal formation. We are ready to set out, and I set my intention to journey to the East.

We travel across the river and come to a large tree. We go up the side of the tree, along a branch, and out into the air. The canoe follows the air currents for some time, while I look around the unfamiliar territory.

The quality of the light is such that I can see tiny bits of dust and other particles suspended in the air. I look more closely and the tiny bits begin to move and surround the canoe. Still in the canoe, we are lifted and carried by these tiny iridescent particles. We are bathed in them. I can feel them going up my nose, and it tickles. I laugh and I feel light fill my nose. I feel like I am expanding. I look at my hands; they have become iridescent like the particles.

Soon I no longer have a distinct form. My rational mind flutters with fear, but it dissipates when I look to my guide the Peacock, and he winks at me. The canoe and everyone in it have dissolved, and we are floating in the air with the rest of the particles. "All one," I think. There is no distinction between them and me. My heart races as I wonder how I will get back together again. I know this is not a relevant question but my rational mind keeps intruding into the experience. Consciously, I breathe deeply and I feel more calm.

I am just a witness, I think. Then I notice that there is a pulse that connects all the other particles with me. I inhale, and they contract toward me; I exhale, and they move away. I am fascinated by this. I speed up my breath and they speed up too. "Fascinating," I think. My physical being has an effect upon our interconnectedness. I take a long slow breath, and slowly the particles move toward me. My exhalation sends them away. I puff and blow to see the effect.

I notice a denser gathering of the particles in the air. I am curious. I see one dark spot in the middle of the particles. The particles are surrounding this dark bit and isolating it from the others. I sit back and watch. Part of me wants to intercede, but I just notice this desire and do nothing. Small particles come up to the dark one, and seem to give it some of their radiance. It lightens over time, and then as I watch it disappears – bing! – and is gone.

The other particles gather around in a ring and pulse in unison. The ring becomes smaller and smaller until there is no middle at all. The empty place has been filled.

I notice that the inner ring of particles has a tiny red dot on one of its edges. Somehow they have been changed. I want to make sense of this and bring it back to my world, but there is no way for me to do this. I have only the experience in my consciousness at this time. All the particles move away from me. I worry that my thoughts of bringing them back to my world have put them off somehow. I am aware that I am now using my rational mind in a place where it has no place.

With this thought, I begin to separate from the particles. I notice that my form is reemerging. Once again I am me. My guides reappear and are standing with me. I am in the boat and we have returned to my river. I thank my guides and the journey ends.

Aho

Interpreting the Journey

Remember that the following interpretations are mine only, and you are free to agree or disagree with them. You may find meanings in the journey that I do not even mention. This is good! Each journey contains many layers, many textures, and many meanings.

From the Warrior, who shows up and is ready for action:

I show up when I consciously take a deep breath to calm my fear. A Warrior needs to manage her fear so it does not prevent her from readiness to act. Calm is necessary for right action.

I show up when I puff and blow the particles around, noticing that I have an effect on them and that my actions have consequences.

I show up by noticing my surroundings throughout the journey. Even if it is not necessary for me to act, I am on "high alert." I pay attention. Awareness, both of internal and external factors, is an extremely important facet of Warrior energy.

- Where did you notice me "show up" in my journey?

From the Teacher, who knows that every journey has a lesson:

I learn that to use my rational mind "in a place where it has no place" does not serve me. If I had interceded and tried to "make sense" of the events in the journey, or done things in a logical way, the journey would have been very different.

I learn how to manage my fear. I consciously use my breath. I look to my guide or leader for reassurance, and receive it in the form of a wink.

I learn that thinking may separate me from others. I separate from the particles as soon as I begin to think. Ivory-tower intellectuals may store knowledge, up there in the air, but they are also isolated. I learn that I can have more connection when I come from my heart and not my head.

A profound teaching is found when I dissolve and then reemerge, complete and whole. I see that I can surrender, break apart, and still not lose myself.

- Where did you see a lesson in my journey?

From the Healer, who recognizes that every journey has healing potential:

There is a healing when the particles give off radiance and then gather together to pulse in unison. They are showing me that there is no division between them, or between them and me.

I am healed when I merge with the particles and become one with them. The literal meaning of heal is "become whole," and this is what happens in this journey.

There is a healing when I express gratitude to my guides. Gratitude completes the circle. You are not whole until you honor those who have helped you.

- Where did you notice a healing in my journey?

From the Magician, who translates insight into application:

To remind myself of this journey, I could find beads with red dots that remind me of the particles in the journey, and place a bowl of them on a table.

An action might be to learn to manage my breath. I might take a yoga class, or learn to meditate. Or I might just sit someplace quiet and listen to myself breathe.

Another action might be to practice doing things that "make no sense," as I did when I felt the light in my nose. I could try to smell the color blue, for instance. Zen Buddhists use this technique, the koan, as an aid to spiritual awakening.

I could ask myself some soul searching questions, such as "When have I held back my emotions fearing that I would lose myself forever?"

- Where did you see an action that might be taken from the insights in this journey?

Some symbols and metaphors present in this journey:

There are many symbols of the East present in this journey. My rational mind continually intrudes into the experience, trying to analyze or "make sense" of what is happening. There are several "airy" words in the journey – fluttering, floating, lifting, dissipating, vanishing, suspending. The canoe travels on the air currents. I am dependent on my breath. In fact, my breath controls the experience. Although I meet no birds here, my eastern landscape is dominated by cultural beliefs about the East.

- What symbols did you see in my journey? What universal, cultural, or personal meanings do they have for you?

Interpret Your Own Journey

Now it's your turn to interpret your own journey to the East. Reread the notes you took after your journey. Ask yourself questions from each perspective. If you can, share your journey with others. Let them give you their interpretations. Listen.

• From the Warrior, who shows up and is ready for action – where did you show up in your journey? What actions did you take?

• From the Teacher, who knows that every story has a lesson and seeks to find it in the journey – where did you notice a lesson in your journey?

• From the Healer, who recognizes that every event has a potential for healing – where did you notice a healing in your journey?

• From the Magician, who translates spiritual insight into practical applications – what is a "real life" application of the insights you received in your journey?

• What are the symbols you noticed in your journey? What universal, cultural, or personal meanings do they have for you?

Aho

Journey to the South

The South is often associated with heat. When we talk about the "southern lands," we mean they are hot. Therefore, the time of day corresponding to the South is noon, when the sun is at its zenith. When we journey to the South we may find ourselves in a desert, or in the top of a palm tree, in a sauna, or other places symbolizing heat. You may find yourself sweating.

The time of year associated with the South is summer, so you may see elements in your journey that remind you of that season: swimming pools and beach balls, for instance.

During the summer we winnow our crops. After your plants have germinated and sprouted, you must nourish and nurture the stronger seedlings, and pare away the weaker. This takes heart connection, and the ability to let go. The South is all about paring down to the essentials.

South is where the element of fire reigns. Fire razes away the old, to allow new growth to flourish. A forest fire destroys, but it also nourishes the soil. Fire reduces all to the basic element of earth, carbon. In your journeys, you may see flames, ovens, ashes, candles, or other things that symbolize fire.

The South rules passion, physical desire, and spontaneity. When we want something very badly, we say we "burn" with desire. In your journeys to the South, you may find yourself drooling with anticipation. You may feel excited. You may feel "on fire" with delight.

The animals that I most closely associate with the South are the snake, who pares down by shedding her old skin; and the coyote, who in many legends falls victim to his own burning and unchecked desires. In other traditions, the South relates to the horse, the spider, or the alligator. Other people may feel the South is the home of the big cats, who live in the hot lands of Africa.

Again, there are no "right" or "wrong" correspondences. In your journey you will visit *your* South, which is like no other.

Other common correspondences of the South include the astrological signs of Aries, Leo, and Sagittarius; the suit of Wands in the Tarot; the First Quarter Moon; and the colors red and orange.

Let us journey to the South to see what the South has for you.

Aho

Journey to the South

Here is a brief recap of the steps into your journey. A complete explanation of these steps is found in Part One, *How to Journey.*

Step One: Smudge

Place a slow-burning plant material such as cedar or sage in a natural holder such as an abalone shell. Light the material and fan the smoke over you and the room with a feather or your hand. It is the symbolism that is important, so if smoke bothers you do not light the plant material, just pretend to do so.

Step Two: Set Sacred Space

In the space where you are journeying, place seven candles on the floor or on a table. Place one candle in the East, one in the South, one in the West, and one in the North. Place three candles in the middle, one each for Sky Father, Earth Mother, and Creator. Call in the directions as they are outlined in Part One, *How to Journey.*

Take a deep breath.

Step Three: Set Your Intention

Set your intention to visit the South. Say, either aloud or to yourself: "Show me what I need to know about the South."

Step Four: Get Comfortable

Arrange yourself comfortably, either lying or sitting. Nearby have your journey journal, pen and Practical Shamanism mp3 available (go to www.shielabaker.com to get your copy). Cover yourself with a blanket if you wish. Cover your eyes with a scarf, and dim the lights.

Step Five: The Journey

Turn on the Practical Shamanism mp3. Follow the instructions on the mp3. If you do not have this mp3, you may listen to other monotonous sounds such as drums, rattles, or chimes, or simply remain in silence. Then imagine placing yourself in a spirit canoe, and that's a birchbark canoe. On your right-hand side, invite your male ancestors, however they show up: two-legged, four-legged, creepy-crawlers, swimmers, winged ones, the standing people, the trees, the rock nation, or any configuration thereof. On your left-hand side, invite your female ancestors, however they show up. In the stern behind you, place your protection, whatever that is for you. In the bow of your boat, invite your spirit guide. State your intention again. And so it begins. Witness what happens.

Step Six: Record Your Journey

Once you have completed your journey, take a few minutes to write down all that you have experienced. Be as specific as possible. Remember your senses – what did it look like, smell like, sound like, feel like, taste like? Don't worry about punctuation, spelling, or grammar. Don't be judgmental about yourself, your writing ability, or the "quality" of your journey. This is not great literature. You don't need to write the next great novel. Simply tell the story.

Step Seven: Give Thanks

Many beings have taken their time and energy to assist you in your quest. Be kind and considerate and thank them for their wisdom and guidance, courage and humor. Give thanks as it is outlined in Part One, *How to Journey*.

Sharing and Witnessing the Journey

Remember it is a powerful thing to share your journeys with others, and to witness theirs in return. Here is my journey to the South. It will become your journey as well as mine.

Shiela's Journey to the South

I am standing in my canoe with my arms outstretched. From my right, Bear swims out to meet me. On my left is Grandmother with young children dancing joyously around her in a circle. Peacock screeches as he arrives to journey with us. In the stern are my three crystals, providing protection. I set my intention to journey to the South, saying, "Show me what I need to know about the South."

I remain standing as the boat slowly and smoothly rises up off the water. We are carried softly in the air, following the route of the river. This is a very gentle cruise. The canoe gains some altitude and we rise up and out of the canyon. The temperature rises as we do. We continue to rise above a mesa, and now we are floating in the wind currents. Still rising, we are being drawn to the right. The bow of the canoe is not pointed toward the right; instead we are moving sideways. In the distance I see what looks like a forest on the horizon.

The wind changes as we drift slowly right. The temperature rises even more; it is becoming very warm. There is a slight turbulence as we travel over the forest. Looking down, I can see all the trees are conifers. At this height I can see the curve of the earth. It gets even warmer.

Now we seem to be on a giant roller-coaster track; I see myself standing in the boat going sideways over the curve of the earth. The clouds are above me and below is the earth. I observe myself and my crew going all around the world, and I marvel that we do not fall out. We return to the place where we began. Then we turn right again and do the same, thus coming full circle. We travel in the canoe over and over to make a bow. I tell myself how silly this sounds.

My rational mind wants to stop and make sense of this. But I quell it and just allow the journey to proceed. There is a long period of nothing. Just waiting, and then waiting some more.

Finally, a serpent shows her head at the bow of the boat. We gaze into each other's eyes. It feels like a meeting of souls. She is not afraid of me and I do not fear her. I feel only deep knowing and trust. I am surprised to find myself trusting a snake. I wrap my arms around her head and hold her tight. She almost purrs. We are long-lost friends, reunited once more. I ask about the roller-coaster track and traveling around the perimeter of the world. Snake says that we needed to do that in order to protect the people.

Snake licks my face and tickles my ears. I laugh as she envelops me in her coils. She tells me that I will need her soon, as there is much change happening. I will need to wrap myself in her. She shows me what is too tight, what is too loose, and what is just right.

I no longer see my guides. Snake and I are alone, suspended in the universe, out beyond the earth. We are just hanging in the sky. We travel together far, far out, slithering among the stars and other galaxies. The drumbeat slows and I ride Snake back to the roller-coaster track. I get back into the canoe and thank my guides. The journey ends.

Aho

Interpreting the Journey

Remember that the following interpretations are mine only, and you are free to agree or disagree with them. You may find meanings in the journey that I do not even mention. Great! Each journey contains many layers, many textures, and many meanings.

From the Warrior, who shows up and is ready for action:

I show up when I begin the journey standing, in the position of the "lookout." I am vigilant and protective of my "crew," as I pay close attention to my surroundings.

I show up when Snake and I tie a bow around the world to "protect the people." In this journey there is an expansiveness – I have traveled out into space and claimed that territory as my own. My role is to protect it.

- Where did you notice me "show up" in my journey?

From the Teacher, who knows that every journey has a lesson:

I am once again taught patience, as I spend much time just waiting. This lesson shows up again and again in my journeys. Patience is important for everyone, but is a particularly hard lesson for me. I have always been a person who wants things to happen *right now*. I want movement, change, interest, and excitement. Learning to simply observe and not "do" has been one of the most beneficial lessons of my life. But I still need reminding!

Snake teaches me to be open to receive help. I can't do it all alone. I need Snake's wisdom and energy to do my best work.
I learn that there are many ways to approach things. My canoe travels to the destination sideways, not straight ahead. Similarly, snakes do not move in a straight line. It is important to understand

which approach is appropriate to the situation. Snake also teaches me what is "too loose, too tight, and just right." She is teaching me appropriateness.

- Where did you see a lesson in my journey?

From the Healer who recognizes that every journey has healing potential:

I heal myself by wrapping my arms around Snake and holding her tight. I listen to her purr.

Purring, a vibration from the chest area, is one of the most healing sounds we can imagine.

I am healed when Snake reciprocates my touch, enveloping me in her coils. She protects, warms, and soothes me. I am held in her loving embrace. She tickles me and licks my face, showing me how much I am loved.

Snake and I recognize each other as old friends. We have come home to one another. We laugh together, in pure joy. It is a huge healing to give and receive love at the same time. This healing gift is mine in this journey.

- Where did you notice a healing in my journey?

From the Magician, who translates insight into application:

Actions I could take to concretize this journey include wearing a snake bracelet, hanging up a photograph of a snake, carving a stick into the shape of a snake, or even getting a snake tattoo!

Since in this journey I was shown the benefit of patience, I could practice waiting. I could arrive early for an appointment. While waiting, I could observe my surroundings.

I could ask myself soul searching questions, such as: Where would it be better to take a sideways approach to something? Am I wrapped up in something? Is it loving and nurturing?

Snake told me I would need her soon, because there is much change happening. I can be alert to changes in my life. How can I apply Snake energy to these changes?

- Where did you see an action that I might take from the insights in this journey?

Some symbols and metaphors present in my journey:

Tying a bow around the world is a metaphor for seeing the earth as a gift. It is a great present from Spirit, and we must cherish it. It needs our protection.

The most obvious symbol in this journey is Snake. The power of Snake medicine is the power of Creation itself. Snake lets go of old skins, of old expectations and desires, and portends coming changes.

Snakes have long been associated with feminine wisdom. In the western world, snakes have been associated with evil, as the snake in the Garden of Eden. St. Patrick was said to have chased the snakes out of Ireland, symbolizing Christianity triumphing over paganism. The symbol of healing medicine, the caduceus, is two entwined snakes. The Hindus think of kundalini energy as a snake. It is safe to say that Snake is one of the most powerful animal symbols. There are so many symbolic meanings for snake, you are sure to find one that resonates with you.

- What symbols did you see in my journey? What universal, cultural, or personal meanings do they have for you?

Interpret Your Own Journey

Now it's your turn to interpret your own journey to the South. Reread the notes you took after your journey. Ask yourself questions from each perspective. If you can, share your journey with others. Let them give you their interpretations. Listen.

• From the Warrior, who shows up and is ready for action – where did you show up in your journey? What actions did you take?
• From the Teacher, who knows that every story has a lesson and seeks to find it in the journey – where did you notice a lesson in your journey?

• From the Healer, who recognizes that every event has a potential for healing –– where did you notice a healing in your journey?

• From the Magician, who translates spiritual insight into practical applications –– what is a "real life" application of the insights you received in your journey?

• What are the symbols you noticed in your journey? What universal, cultural, or personal meanings do they have for you?

Aho

Journey to the West

For me, the West represents the Great Mystery, or the realm of the unknown. The time of day corresponds to dusk, or sunset, when the shadows begin to fall. The season associated with the West is autumn, the time of harvest. We gather and reap the earth's bounty and prepare for the dark time. Gateways between the worlds may be found in the West.

The West is the realm of water, a medium at once alien and vital to our species. We cannot breathe under water, yet over ninety percent of our bodies consist of this valuable fluid. In your journey to the West you may find yourself near, or in, lakes, rivers, streams, ponds, or oceans. You may find that you *can* breathe underwater. When you journey to the West, you become like a deep-sea diver searching for emotional treasure buried beneath the waves.

The West rules the emotions and the unconscious, so when we visit the West we are asking to have things brought from the depths of the unconscious into the light of consciousness. During your journey you may find yourself weeping, laughing, raging, or swept by any of a thousand strong emotions. You may remember events you thought you had forgotten long ago. You may feel the emotions of childhood loss or joy.

The animals often associated with the West are all the swimmers and sea creatures, and for me, the bear. Many people "see" water creatures when they visit the West – trout, salmon, crabs, lobsters, dolphins, whales, carp, even jellyfish. But not everyone will experience this. For me, the bear has appeared in the West many times and has given me profound insights into feelings and events long buried in my unconscious. Remember that the landscapes you are discovering are yours. Although affected by your cultural symbolism, you need not be directed by it. You are unique.

Other correspondences of the West include the astrological signs of Cancer, Scorpio, and Pisces; the suit of Cups in the Tarot; the

Full Moon and time of illumination; and the color blue. Let us journey to the West to see what the West has for you.

Aho

Journey to the West

Here is a brief recap of the steps into your journey. A complete explanation of these steps is found in Part One, *How to Journey.*

Step One: Smudge

Place a slow-burning plant material such as cedar or sage in a natural holder such as an abalone shell. Light the material and fan the smoke over you and the room with a feather or your hand. It is the symbolism that is important, so if smoke bothers you do not light the plant material, just pretend to do so.

Step Two: Set Sacred Space

In the space where you are journeying, place seven candles on the floor or on a table. Place one candle in the East, one in the South, one in the West, and one in the North. Place three candles in the middle, one each for Sky Father, Earth Mother, and Creator. Call in the directions as they are outlined in Part One, *How to Journey.*

Take a deep breath.

Step Three: Set Your Intention

Set your intention to visit the West. Say, either aloud or to yourself: "Show me what I need to know about the West."

Step Four: Get Comfortable

Arrange yourself comfortably, either lying or sitting. Nearby have your journey journal, pen and Practical Shamanism mp3 available (go to www.shielabaker.com to get your copy). Cover yourself with a blanket if you wish. Cover your eyes with a scarf, and dim the lights.

Step Five: The Journey

Turn on the Practical Shamanism mp3. Follow the instructions on the mp3. If you do not have this mp3, you may listen to other monotonous sounds such as drums, rattles, or chimes, or simply remain in silence. Then imagine placing yourself in a spirit canoe, and that's a birchbark canoe. On your right-hand side, invite your male ancestors, however they show up: two-legged, four-legged, creepy-crawlers, swimmers, winged ones, the standing people, the trees, the rock nation, or any configuration thereof. On your left-hand side, invite your female ancestors, however they show up. In the stern behind you, place your protection, whatever that is for you. In the bow of your boat, invite your spirit guide. State your intention again. And so it begins. Witness what happens.

Step Six: Record Your Journey

Once you have completed your journey, take a few minutes to write down all that you have experienced. Be as specific as possible. Remember your senses – what did it look like, smell like, sound like, feel like, taste like? Don't worry about punctuation, spelling, or grammar. Don't be judgmental about yourself, your writing ability, or the "quality" of your journey. This is not great literature. You don't need to write the next great novel. Simply tell the story.

Step Seven: Give Thanks

Give thanks as it is outlined in Part One, *How to Journey.*

Sharing and Witnessing the Journey

Remember it is a powerful thing to share your journeys with others, and to witness theirs in return. Here is my journey to the West. It has become your journey as well as mine.

Shiela's Journey to the West

I am sitting in my canoe feeling tired. I take a deep breath and wait. I stretch and look over to my right, where Bear is stretching too. Heeding my call, he ambles to the shore and gingerly gets into the water. He swims toward me, seeming at home in the water. On my left Grandmother is also stretching, like she is just waking up. She is wearing white robes and I am suddenly struck by her beauty, which I had not noticed before. Her robe is long and trails behind her as she approaches the shore. At the edge of the water she steps onto the water rather than into it. She seems to be floating on top of the water. I am entranced, watching her come closer. She settles into her outrigger, which is attached to the left side of my canoe. In the bow of the canoe is Peacock. He is observing Bear and Grandmother. I am not sure when or how he got into the boat. Behind me as always are the three crystals, my protection.

I stand and set my intention to journey to the West. I am not sure why it is important for me to stand, but I know that I must. Peacock shudders and his eyes become alert. The canoe jerks away from the shore and I feel unsteady, although I remain standing.

We jerk along for some time. I remain standing, witnessing the jerking. I realize that something is holding us back; we do not move beyond a certain distance. I am curious about this but remain standing, looking forward. We remain in the same place, not moving ahead at all.

I feel tethered, as if I was at the end of a leash. I think, "I must be at the end of my rope." I just wait and watch the time go by. No one else seems disturbed and I settle down, watching and waiting for something, although I am not sure what. The landscape begins to move, passing by as we remain stationary. This is a strange sensation. I think it may be an illusion. I am still standing as the canyon walls pass by.

Ahead I see a vast expanse opening before us. The walls recede and we are in open space. Now I observe from above the scene. I am aware of the largeness of the foreground; open, clear and undefined. No features stand out. I take a deep breath and look around, opening my arms to my sides. I feel open, clear, and free. I am not sure whether I am alone, but I only want to look forward rather than around to see who is with me. I don't even see Peacock ahead of me. I rise up, arms outstretched. Then I begin to twirl, round and round, but so slowly that I do not get dizzy. I enjoy the sensation and laugh. I feel ease.

I become curious. I wonder, "what if?" I move my hands slightly to see what will happen. Nothing changes. I know I am to wait to see what the West has for me. My arms tire and I drop them to my sides. I am suspended above the river. I can see the mesa I often visit, but I am not drawn there although I can see activity that might interest me at other times. I remain floating above the river. I wait a long time and a memory rises in my mind, of my mother chiding me for impatience. "Ha!" I think, "if only she could see me now." This is my rational mind talking. I quiet myself by breathing and I am still floating above the river.

A desire awakens in me to make things happen. I notice this desire, mostly without judgment. I wonder "what if" again. What if I imagined a stairwell and climbed it? So I climb imaginary stairs but I don't go anywhere. I tire of this and stop. I am just waiting again.

Suddenly I am turned upside down. I hang in space, upside down and dangling. I am swinging slightly and I think, "This is fun." My robes do not drop over my head, but remain as they would if I were standing. How interesting. More time passes and I think that if this were ordinary reality I would be getting bored by now. I notice I can't stop thinking.

Yep, I'm just hanging around. Then I ask, "What is the West to me?" I look down, toward the river to see what's going on there. Grandmother is standing in her outrigger where she often journeys with me, and Bear is splashing around in the water, playing with an Otter. They are tossing a shell between them and seem to be enjoying themselves. They are a long way down. I don't see Peacock at all.

I'm still hanging upside down and all is well below. Then I wonder about above. Looking up I see stars in the daytime sky. The daylight is clear and bright, but I can still see the stars. No sun or moon is visible. I am still upside down. I consciously focus on my breath. I notice this makes me feel more open, calmer. I was not aware that I was holding my breath. I feel much better when I notice my breath. I let out a sigh and feel relief. A sense of deep longing wells up and I feel tears in back of my eyes. While I do not cry, I notice. A longer, deeper sigh escapes me and I feel an enormous spaciousness in my being, as though my body isn't taking up all the space in my skin.

As I exhale, I feel an odd sensation. A part of me is leaving my body. I have no fear, just openness. I have more room in my body because I'm not taking up all the space. I sigh even more, feeling lighter and lighter. Then I notice that the body (no longer mine) is becoming like a veil, thinning out over the horizon. Cool experience!

Back in my body, I notice that I am stretching out over the river and the mesa and everywhere. Each breath takes me further out into the void. Thinning and thinning more. I have become like gauze over the world. I notice that there is no *me*. I am the wind that touches the leaf, that is the tree, that is the sap, that is the earth, that is.

I think, "Weird." But the feeling doesn't stop because I am thinking! It goes on and on. Some part of me weeps with joy. I do not have to go anywhere, do anything, or be anything. *I am*. My crying continues, but then subsides. It is replaced by breathing and being. Quiet, quiet, quiet. No more tears.

Breathing, breathing, breathing. My eyes are closed, moist with tears. *I am*, upside down, then right side up.

And then I am in my canoe, standing. Grandmother is in her outrigger and Bear plays quietly with Otter in the water. Peacock takes his head out from under his wing and gazes at me. "Ready to go home?" he asks. I nod and we are back at the shore of my river.

Aho

Interpreting the Journey

Remember that the following interpretations are mine only, and you are free to agree or disagree with them. You may find meanings in the journey that I do not even mention. Great! Each journey contains many layers, many textures, many meanings.

From the Warrior, who shows up and is ready for action:

When the journey is long, as this one is, the aspect of the Warrior may be present in many places, and it can be overwhelming to name each one. This is okay. Work with the ones that are important to you right now. Often when we revisit journeys, new aspects occur to us, ready to present us with their wisdom.

I show up when I know that I must stand, without knowing why. I remain standing even though the canoe is unsteady. I stand my ground, and it is important to know when this is necessary.

I show up when I start to wonder "what if." This is the beginning of strategizing, which is an aspect of the Warrior.

I show up when I maintain my calm when I am suddenly turned upside down. I am open to whatever happens, not attached to what I think "should" happen. I do not force things to happen.

- Where did you notice me "show up" in my journey?

From the Teacher, who knows that every journey has a lesson:

I learn that I do not have to be anything or do anything. I just *am*. I do not have to move or go anywhere. In fact, I am hanging upside down and unable to go anywhere.

- When I am turned upside down, I learn that looking at things from a different perspective can be enlightening.

When I notice that there is no me – that I am the wind and the trees – I learn that my definition of self does not have to be limited. The lesson is that I am infinite.

And here again I am being taught patience! A memory surfaces in this journey from my childhood, when I was scolded for my impatience. I am given a chance to show that I have now learned this lesson. I *can* wait.

- Where did you see a lesson in my journey?

From the Healer, who recognizes that every journey has healing potential:

There is a healing when I notice that feeling doesn't stop even though I am thinking. My rational mind and emotions co-exist in the same space. When thinking and feeling come together there is a tremendous release of pressure. I do not have to be at war within myself.

I experience healing when I allow myself to experience my emotions fully. I both weep and leap with joy. I let the feelings wash over me, without trying to curb them in any way.

At the end of the journey I experience a period of intense quiet, when all I notice is my own breath. Tension and stress are totally gone.

- Where did you notice a healing in my journey?

From the Magician, who translates insight into application:

I spend some time in this journey being upside down, and observing the world from this unfamiliar perspective. I could try this "at home" by hanging my head over the edge of the bed or couch, and observing what I see. What differences do I notice? Or I could turn the pictures on my walls upside down, and look at them closely. What do I see from this perspective?

In the journey I say, "I am the wind that touches the leaf...." To build on this insight, I could do a writing exercise in which I describe myself in natural terms. I could write ten to twenty sentences, all beginning with "I am" and finishing with a natural metaphor. Writing exercises are a great way to concretize, enhance and expand the messages from a journey.

I could ask myself soul searching questions suggested by the journey, such as "Where do I feel at the end of my rope?" or "Where, when or how has my life been turned upside down?

- Where did you see an action that might be taken from the insights in my journey?

Some symbols and metaphors present in my journey:

The West symbolizes the Great Mystery and is the home of paradox. The meaning of this journey is that there may not be a meaning. Nothing I do in this journey has any effect upon the outcome. This can be threatening, but it can also be liberating.

There is an Otter in this journey. The Otter symbolizes playfulness, and is often about female energy. The female Otter and the male ancestor, the Bear, play together in the water. This symbolizes harmonious relations between the sexes when we allow ourselves to play and have fun.

The stars being visible in the daytime sky is a symbol for seeing what I am not usually able to see. Because I am upside down, my perception has been altered, and I let go of thinking that I know how things ought to be.

A symbol in this journey is likewise turned upside down. At the end of the journey I find that Peacock has been asleep with his head tucked under his wing, but Peacock symbolizes wakefulness because of his many eyes that never close.

- What symbols and meanings did you see in my journey? What universal, cultural, or personal meanings do they have for you?

Interpret Your Own Journey

Now it's your turn to interpret your own journey to the West. Reread the notes you took after your journey. Ask yourself questions from each perspective. If you can, share your journey with others. Let them give you their interpretations. Listen.

- From the Warrior, who shows up and is ready for action – where did you show up in your journey? What actions did you take?

• From the Teacher, who knows that every story has a lesson and seeks to find it in the journey – where did you notice a lesson in your journey?

• From the Healer, who recognizes that every event has a potential for healing – where did you notice a healing in your journey?

• From the Magician, who translates spiritual insight into practical applications – what is a "real life" application of the insights you received in your journey?

• What are the symbols you noticed in your journey? What universal, cultural, or personal meanings do they have for you?

Aho

Journey to the North

With this, our journey to the North, we complete our initial journeys to the four compass directions. Be aware that these first journeys have only "scratched the surface" of the richness waiting for you in these realms. You may come back again and again, and each time you will be rewarded with new insights and new wisdom. Visit often.

In my tradition, the North is associated with the night, when all is dark and still. The journeys you take to the North may place you in darkness. Your visual sense may be muted, and your other senses more acute. The North is associated with the season of winter. You may notice snow or ice, or other symbolic representations of winter in your journey. The winter is a time for conserving our energy, being thoughtful, ruminating on what we have learned, and making plans for the coming spring. Winter is about being quiet and listening to our inner wisdom. It is about learning what to release, and what to embrace.

The North is represented by the element of earth, and the material, physical world. Don't be surprised if the rocks speak to you in your journeys to the North. You may dig in the dirt. You may go into caves. You may travel down tunnels into the bowels of the earth. The plant world may seem more alive, more conscious.

Groundedness, stability, and patience are attributes associated with the North. The North is where we access ancestral wisdom, the deep knowing that cannot be "rationally explained." When we are patient and willing to sit quietly, ruminating and listening, ancient wisdom is available for our access. Ancestral wisdom does not appear when we are running about, flapping wildly. It comes to those who wait for it.

The animals associated with the North are ground dwellers such as moles and groundhogs, and migratory beasts such as caribou, buffalo, or elk, who know when to travel to the sweet water and when to come back again. Ruled by instinctual deep knowing, they show us how it is done. If you need answers to the important questions for your life, it is good to journey to the North to find those deep knowing places, and awaken your ancestral wisdom.

Other correspondences of the North include the astrological signs of Taurus, Virgo, and Capricorn; the suit of Pentacles in the Tarot; the Dark Moon and the time of invisibility and trust; and the color white, like the snow in the vast expanse of the far North.

Let us journey to the North to see what the North has for you.

Aho

Journey to the North

Here is a brief recap of the steps into your journey. A complete explanation of these steps is found in Part One, *How to Journey.*

Step One: Smudge

Place a slow-burning plant material such as cedar or sage in a natural holder such as an abalone shell. Light the material and fan the smoke over you and the room with a feather or your hand. It is the symbolism that is important, so if smoke bothers you do not light the plant material, just pretend to do so.

Step Two: Set Sacred Space

In the space where you are journeying, place seven candles on the floor or on a table. Place one candle in the East, one in the South, one in the West, and one in the North. Place three candles in the middle, one each for Sky Father, Earth Mother, and Creator. Call in the directions as they are outlined in Part One, *How to Journey.*

Take a deep breath.

Step Three: Set Your Intention

Set your intention to visit the North. Say, either aloud or to yourself: "Show me what I need to know about the North."

Step Four: Get Comfortable

Arrange yourself comfortably, either lying or sitting. Nearby have your journey journal, pen and Practical Shamanism mp3 available (go to www.shielabaker.com to get your copy). Cover yourself with a blanket if you wish. Cover your eyes with a scarf, and dim the lights.

Step Five: The Journey

Turn on the Practical Shamanism mp3. Follow the instructions on the mp3. If you do not have this mp3, you may listen to other monotonous sounds such as drums, rattles, or chimes, or simply remain in silence. Then imagine placing yourself in a spirit canoe, and that's a birchbark canoe. On your right-hand side, invite your male ancestors, however they show up: two-legged, four-legged, creepy-crawlers, swimmers, winged ones, the standing people, the trees, the rock nation, or any configuration thereof. On your left-hand side, invite your female ancestors, however they show up. In the stern behind you, place your protection, whatever that is for you. In the bow of your boat, invite your spirit guide. State your intention again. And so it begins. Witness what happens.

Step Six: Record Your Journey

Once you have completed your journey, take a few minutes to write down all that you have experienced. Be as specific as possible. Remember your senses – what did it look like, smell like, sound like, feel like, taste like? Don't worry about punctuation, spelling, or grammar. Don't be judgmental about yourself, your writing ability, or the "quality" of your journey. This is not great literature. You don't need to write the next great novel. Simply tell the story.

Step Seven: Give Thanks

Many beings have witnessed your journey, offering guidance, encouragement, protection and their time and energy, be gracious and thank them. Give thanks as it is outlined in Part One, *How to Journey.*

Sharing and Witnessing the Journey

Remember it is a powerful thing to share your journeys with others, and to witness theirs in return. Here is my journey to the North. It has become your journey as well as mine.

Shiela's Journey to the North

I am sitting in my canoe. My male ancestor, Bear, swims toward me from the right riverbank. On my left Grandmother is sitting at the edge of the water. Peacock stands in the bow looking forward. From the stern my crystals are protecting me. I set my intention: "Show me what the North holds for me."

I do not paddle, but the canoe moves into the current of the river and we are carried along easily. Trees surround the river on both sides. Standing in the bow, Peacock spreads his tail and I am unable to see beyond the multiple eyes. Like Peacock will, he shakes his tail, and as he does all the eyes take flight. They move in the air above and around us. Bear is still swimming along, and I see that Grandmother has settled into her outrigger alongside me. I feel as if we are in a cocoon made of peacock eyes.

The current flows along neither fast nor slow. I hear a roar in the distance but cannot see beyond the eyes. I fear the worst and brace myself for going over a waterfall. But instead the canoe lifts and floats out beyond the falls, landing beyond the turbulence in the middle of smooth water. Moved by some unseen force, the canoe turns and heads into the area behind the falls.

I find myself out of the canoe. My ancestors are not to be seen, nor is my guide with me. Behind the falls is a cave, dark and dank with smooth ledges to walk upon. The walls are iridescent midnight blue. The water flows back into the cave, where it is very cool. I wander back into the cave, noticing that the water becomes more shallow until it is just a small trickle. I smell something unknown. I am aware of a presence. The hairs stand up on my arms. I am on alert. I have a growing sense of some being, somewhere nearby. I feel something move in the depths of the cave.

I feel mesmerized, as if stuck in stone. I become aware of a large creature nearby. I recognize her as a spider. She is very large and hairy but I am not afraid. And she is not afraid of me. Now I notice cocoons lining the walls of the cave, and I identify the smell as rotting flesh. My mind and senses tell me I ought to be afraid and nauseated, but I am not.

The presence of Spider comforts me. She bows to me and offers me a ledge to sit on. We are communicating, but not with words or gestures. She tells me of her journey into the cave; how it is her home and sanctuary. She tells me of those in the other world who were mean to her. She no longer ventures into the realm of light.

As I sit with my legs dangling over a ledge, Spider weaves me a pair of spider-web slippers so my feet will not get cut on the stones on the way out. The slippers are warm and waterproof. I thank her for her gift and leave the cave. The way out is much shorter than the way in.

I return through the falls, and climb back into my canoe. Bear appears on my right all covered in seaweed. On my left Grandmother holds shells in her hands. All around me in the water are lily pads piled high with mangoes, papayas, and other tropical fruits. We take time to swim and gather fruits for our return journey. The drumbeat fades and I return to the physical realm.

Aho

Interpreting the Journey

Remember that the following interpretations are mine only, and you are free to agree or disagree with them. You may find meanings in the journey that I do not even mention. Great! Each journey contains many layers, many textures, and many meanings.

From the Warrior, who shows up and is ready for action:

I show up when I follow the water back into the cave. I am following the clues and using all my senses to discern my surroundings. My senses are heightened, including the sense of "deep knowing" when I sense the presence of Spider before I can see her.

I show up when I recognize Spider as an ally, not an enemy. I recognize our commonality, and as soon as I do, I am able to define what my senses have been telling me. I identify the smell as rotting flesh, although this does not scare or nauseate me. I know that what serves Spider, serves me.

- Where did you notice me "show up" in my journey?

From the Teacher, who knows that every journey has a lesson:

There is a lesson when Spider tells me her story. Sometimes just the act of showing up allows someone else to share their stories. When we are willing to show up, then we can come together with another. We are enriched and educated by the stories of others. The lesson is that our stories are unique and individual, but at the same time they are all the same.

Spider teaches me about communication. We communicate, but not with words or gestures. There are many ways to communicate, and words and gestures are just two of them. Spider and I communicate psychically and energetically. When I notice these unconscious communications they are brought up to consciousness.

There is a lesson here about graciousness and hospitality. Spider shows me how to make a space for a guest to feel at home. She waited in the background until I was ready to see her. She didn't dragoon me into her lair, or pull me in before I was ready. She let me sit down and get acclimatized. She paid attention to my comfort zone and did not intrude before it was time. Finally, she even gave me a gift.

- Where did you see a lesson in my journey?

From the Healer, who recognizes that every journey has healing potential:

It is healing when Spider bows to me, recognizing me as her ally just as I had recognized her. She honors me. She honors me again by telling me her story. Telling our stories is a powerful act of healing. Not only the storyteller is healed, but so is the listener. That is a primary reason for telling our stories.

The Spider's graciousness heals me by making me feel at home. She invites me inside, she offers me a ledge to sit on, she tells me a story, and finally she gifts me with a pair of slippers she has woven herself. She is personally concerned for my comfort and health. I am bathed in her care. At the end of the journey, I am healed by being offered a joyous celebration, full of warm and juicy tropical fruits. I relax and enjoy myself, for it is time to rejoice. This is also a teaching, of course. It is important to take time to celebrate and rejoice in the bounty of life.

- Where did you notice a healing in my journey?

From the Magician, who translates insight into application:

I am again gifted with protection for my feet in this journey. My journeys often caution me to take care of my feet, because they connect me to my path. Without my feet I cannot journey at all. Therefore I can take practical actions to protect and comfort them: exercise them, massage them, keep them warm, and wear appropriate shoes.

I can pay attention to my non verbal communications. What am I communicating without words or gestures? What are others communicating to me? I can especially pay attention to the communications between me and other species, which are of necessity non verbal. What communications are there for me from birds, insects, fish, or other mammals? I can practice watching other creatures communicate, and learning from their interactions.

Spiders are not hard to find. I could spend some hours watching spiders, and if I can find one weaving a web, that would be especially wonderful. This will both develop my patience and instill awe and respect for this much misunderstood creature.

I can practice my hospitality skills by inviting friends to visit me, and paying attention to their comfort, so their stories will flow forth easily. What preparations can I make so they will feel welcome? What gifts could I offer them?

- Where did you see an action that might be taken from the insights in this journey?

Some symbols and metaphors present in my journey:

Again in this journey the symbolism of peacock eyes is turned upside down. When I am surrounded by the eyes, paradoxically I cannot see at all.

The major symbol in this journey is of course the spider. There are stories, legends, and myths about spiders in nearly every culture. Like the snake, the spider has been maligned for millennia, and for many of the same reasons.

Spiders are often associated with feminine wisdom. Weaving and sewing has been "women's work" back through the mists of time. Spider is the Master Weaver, who draws her material from within herself to create her web. She creates from within her own body, as females do. In many traditions, the spider, known to some as Grandmother Spider, wove the fabric of the universe itself. In other stories Spider created the sticky web of fate, or the tricky web of illusion, in which you may get caught.

Adding to the dimensions of their symbolism, spiders often show up in popular culture: books, movies and even cartoons. Think of *Charlotte's Web*, Shelob's lair in *Lord of the Rings*, The silicon spider in *Star Trek*, *Spider-Man*, the movie *Arachnophobia* and many others.

Spider is an immensely powerful symbol. It is up to me to determine what her meaning is for me. The same is true for you.

- What symbols did you see in my journey? What universal, cultural, or personal meanings do they have for you?

Interpret Your Own Journey

Now it's your turn to interpret your own journey to the North. Reread the notes you took after your journey. Ask yourself questions from each perspective. If you can, share your journey with others. Let them give you their interpretations. Listen.

- From the Warrior, who shows up and is ready for action – where did you show up in your journey? What actions did you take?

• From the Teacher, who knows that every story has a lesson and seeks to find it in the journey – where did you notice a lesson in your journey?

• From the Healer, who recognizes that every event has a potential for healing – where did you notice a healing in your journey?

• From the Magician, who translates spiritual insight into practical applications – what is a "real life" application of the insights you received in your journey?

• What are the symbols you noticed in your journey? What universal, cultural, or personal meanings do they have for you?

Aho

Journey to the Male Ancestor

The next two journeys are to our ancestral archetypes, both masculine and feminine. These journeys help us to answer one of the four powerful journey questions: Where did I come from?

When you journey to your ancestral archetypes, you are asking to be shown what you have to learn from this ancestor. What is there about your personal lineage that is helpful in your daily life? How has it shaped who you are now? What are you willing to carry into your future? The more journeys you make, the more information your ancestors will give you.

Characteristics generally attributed to the masculine archetype may or may not be what you experience in your journeys. This is a personal and intimate interaction. Sometimes your actual relatives, such as a grandfather or uncle or father, may appear to you as your male ancestor in your journey. Or your male ancestor may appear to you as an animal or a rock or a tree. It could be different each time you journey. As you know by now, my male ancestor is a bear, and has been for many years.

Regardless of your gender, getting in touch with your masculine side will give you access to this energy and power. Our male ancestor often helps us put our words into action, and in walking our talk.

Let us discover what your male ancestor may have to show you.

Journey to the Male Ancestor

Here is a brief recap of the steps into your journey. A complete explanation of these steps is found in Part One, *How to Journey*.

Step One: Smudge

Place a slow-burning plant material such as cedar or sage in a natural holder such as an abalone shell. Light the material and fan the smoke over you and the room with a feather or your hand. It is the symbolism that is important, so if smoke bothers you do not light the plant material, just pretend to do so.

Step Two: Set Sacred Space

In the space where you are journeying, place seven candles on the floor or on a table. Place one candle in the East, one in the South, one in the West, and one in the North. Place three candles in the middle, one each for Sky Father, Earth Mother, and Creator. Call in the directions as they are outlined in Part One, *How to Journey*.

Take a deep breath.

Step Three: Set Your Intention

Set your intention to visit your Male Ancestor. Say, either aloud or to yourself: "Show me what I need to know about my Male Ancestor."

Step Four: Get Comfortable

Arrange yourself comfortably, either lying or sitting. Nearby have your journey journal, pen and Practical Shamanism mp3 available (go to www.shielabaker.com to get your copy). Cover yourself with a blanket if you wish. Cover your eyes with a scarf, and dim the lights.

Step Five: The Journey

Turn on the Practical Shamanism mp3. Follow the instructions on the mp3. If you do not have this mp3, you may listen to other monotonous sounds such as drums, rattles, or chimes, or simply remain in silence. Then imagine placing yourself in a spirit canoe, and that's a birchbark canoe. On your right-hand side, invite your male ancestors, however they show up: two-legged, four-legged, creepy-crawlers, swimmers, winged ones, the standing people, the trees, the rock nation, or any configuration thereof. On your left-hand side, invite your female ancestors, however they show up. In the stern behind you, place your protection, whatever that is for you. In the bow of your boat, invite your spirit guide. State your intention again. And so it begins. Witness what happens.

Step Six: Record Your Journey

Once you have completed your journey, take a few minutes to write down all that you have experienced. Be as specific as possible. Remember your senses – what did it look like, smell like, sound like, feel like, taste like? Don't worry about punctuation, spelling, or grammar. Don't be judgmental about yourself, your writing ability, or the "quality" of your journey. This is not great literature. You don't need to write the next great novel. Simply tell the story.

Step Seven: Give Thanks

Our ancestors are powerful allies, they teach us how to be or sometimes how not to be. Either way this is a great gift and is worthy of gratitude. Give thanks as it is outlined in Part One, *How to Journey*.

Sharing and Witnessing the Journey

Remember it is a powerful thing to share your journeys with others, and to witness theirs in return. Here is my journey to the Male Ancestor. It has become your journey as well as mine.

Shiela's Journey to the Male Ancestor

I am standing in the canoe. On my right is Bear; on my left is Grandmother. Bear has a strip of fur shaved off his back, and the exposed skin is studded with gemstones. Grandmother is wearing a white buckskin gown decorated with gems as well. Peacock arrives looking weary, his feathers tattered. The three crystals in the stern are covered with a gauzy shawl.

The boat ascends. We are traveling over the edge of the canyon. I see an intriguing black spot on the top of the canyon, and we travel over to see it. I had assumed that it was a fire pit, but I see now that it is a fissure, a crack in the earth. It has jagged edges and is very dark. We descend into the crack. The air is warm. We continue to descend, deep into the earth. The canoe finally comes to a stop, and we all get out and stand in a circle. The crystals magically come alight and we can see. The walls are a beautiful copper color, reminding me of my kitchen and comforting me. The space we are in is small so we stand close together. We circle the boat and sense a rhythm, which again comforts us. I have a general sense of moving energy, pulsing and warm. This warm energy dispels my usual fears.

One of the walls moves and a passageway opens. I am compelled to go inside. The others follow, until Peacock passes over my shoulder and leads the way. I can hear his wings ahead, but the light gets dimmer as we leave the crystals further behind. The passage narrows as we continue. The walls brush against our arms. Bear and Grandmother are now beside me, one at each shoulder. The energy has shifted slightly; I feel some fear and I am glad for their company.

We continue this way for a long distance. It gets colder, and the walls widen. We come to a great hall. I did not notice any lights until we stepped into the hall, but now all is alive with lights and people. Bustle and mirth fill the air. No one seems to notice us, as if we are invisible.

It takes a moment to get used to the light and recover our bearings. Still no one is paying us any mind. My anxiety and the smell of the feast they are preparing are making me hungry. We approach the food laden tables, at first timidly but then more boldly. This has been a long journey and we are very hungry. I notice that the people are dressed in medieval garb, and I want to approach someone and talk with them, but I am uncertain, a little afraid. But filling my belly seems to decrease my fear. I help myself to a goblet of some unknown liquid and slug it back quickly. I feel myself getting into the party spirit that fills the room.

I notice that the chairs at one end of the room are larger, and I move toward them. I want to see what else is down there. The environment changes as I go down the hall. The plates are larger, the furniture more delicate and refined, and the goblets polished until they sparkle. The women are ornately dressed, with elaborate hairdos.

At the end of the hall there is a being whom I have never seen before: a stag with the hind end of a man. His horns are adorned with flowers and bells, and he wears a necklace of gold with a huge dangling medallion. I feel a difference in myself and look down at my clothing. I see that I am dressed in a lavish white gown. My hair is no longer hanging loose around my shoulders but is swept up on top of my head.

The stag rises and we greet each other in an unusual way. We nuzzle one another. He rubs his scent on me and I rub my cheek along the side of his face. We are old friends. I am there to witness his coronation and to be his consort. He bows before me, and I climb onto his back. The room quiets as we walk the length of the hall.

We go out onto a balcony, and cheering erupts from the crowd below. I get off his back and he stands on his hind legs, his head swinging from side to side. The bells on his antlers jingle. He is delighted with the reception, and the people are almost delirious with joy. I think, "This is very profound!"

I am watching from the sidelines. I see the entire crowd kneel, in obeisance. The Stag turns and we all bow to a statue of the horned goddess. I know I have been brought there to be a physical symbol of this goddess. Fear arises as I wonder if they will sacrifice me, but once again I remind myself to just watch.

The Stag again offers me his back, and I climb upon it. We go back into the hall where now the tone is somber. I seem to be the focus now, and once again I feel fear. We come to a big altar, and I ascend to its top. The drink I had is beginning to have an effect on me. I am dizzy, and my eyes are not focusing. I feel giddy and excited, although in the back of my mind I think I should be afraid. The altar stone is cold but I don't mind. Something inside of me is wanting out, and I feel a stirring inside me.

The Stag once again nuzzles me and I am fond with him. Someone comes to the table, and although I feel nothing my abdomen is opened and a small creature is lifted out of me. There is much cheering, and I smile. This little being is half-stag and half-human. I have been carrying her for some time unknowing.

I get up and the Stag again offers his back. The wet nurses have taken the tiny being and I am no longer needed. The Stag delivers me back to my guides. We leave the hall and I find myself in the canoe at the edge of my stream where we began the journey.

Aho

Interpreting the Journey

Remember that the following interpretations are mine only, and you are free to agree or disagree with them. You may find meanings in the journey that I do not even mention. Good! Each journey contains many layers, many textures, and many meanings.

From the Warrior, who shows up and is ready for action:

I show up when I become hungry upon smelling the feast, and I take action to care for myself. When I do, my fear decreases. I didn't stay in fear but took action to decrease it.

I showed up when I remained focused on my desires, and kept on task. I didn't get distracted or thrown off by the revelry and color and movement that is so prevalent in this journey. I came into the hallway, went where I needed to go, and did what I needed to do.

I also took steps to become the consort and I gave birth to a new generation in spite of my fear. This exemplifies the female warrior. I act in spite of fear, and I do not get caught up in the accolades, which are not for me.

• Where did you notice me "show up" in my journey?

From the Teacher, who knows that every journey has a lesson:

I am taught that when I "pull back and just watch," my fear dissipates. I learn that fear is anticipation of pain, not pain itself.

I learn that I can eat, drink, and be merry and also stay focused and on task.

I learn how to accept honor without succumbing to egotism. I don't let the cheering and reverence lead me into arrogance.

I change my attire in this journey, dressing in finery and wearing an elaborate hairdo. I am dressing to match my consort, the Stag, who wears bells and a medallion. I am taught when it is appropriate and necessary to dress regally.

After the birth, the small being is taken away and I am no longer needed. The lesson here is about letting go, and knowing when to do so. My function is complete, and hers is just beginning. But I am not part of her story, and this is something I need to accept. This is a lesson all parents must learn when their children grow up.

- Where did you see a lesson in my journey?

From the Healer, who recognizes that every journey has healing potential:

I receive a healing in this journey around food. As a child, my parents were ashamed of me because I was a chubby little girl. When we had company, I was not allowed to eat the "party food." But here in this journey I eat and drink all I want without shame. The copper walls remind me of my own kitchen now, which is warm and comforting.

It was healing for me to allow myself to be carried by the Stag, in spite of my propensity to be independent and "do it all myself." I was able to lean on his strength, again without shame or negative judgment of myself.

It was healing to give birth and be lightened in the process, and be treated with such reverence. When I was no longer needed for this function I was given back to my guides and ancestors with honor. When we are honored for something worthy we have done, many wounds of neglect and abuse close for good. I am acknowledged by the Stag and the crowd as an important person, but without feeling "puffed up." Instead I feel blessed.

- Where did you notice a healing in my journey?

From the Magician, who translates insight into application:

This journey is full of celebration and revelry. One action I could take would be to throw myself a party, celebrating an achievement or honor, birthday, or other occasion. I could dress up in fancy clothes, and serve luxurious food and drink. Although there is no need to get drunk, I could have a glass of champagne and notice the effect it has on me.

Soul searching questions I could ask myself include: "Where have I completed something and am no longer needed?" "What have I brought to birth and can now let go of?" "Where in my life do I feel like the queen?" No one creates on their own, so "who is my consort? How do I honor him? How do I let him honor me?" "How well do I accept honors? Do I preen and let it go to my head, or can I accept it for the healing gift it is?"

Although I am not the kind of person who would like a mounted stag's head trophy on my wall, I could get a statue or picture of a stag and put it in a place of honor, such as on an altar. I could hang flowers and bells in the statue's antlers, or place a vase of flowers underneath the picture.

- Where did you see an action that might be taken from the insights in this journey?

Some symbols and metaphors present in my journey:

In ancient Anglo-Saxon culture, the Stag was revered as a symbol of power and high status. Kings and noble families often appropriated this symbol for their own territory or clan. In nearly every culture which had a relationship with antlered beasts, the Stag stood as a symbol of masculine pride and true-hearted dignity. This symbol is also highly personal for me, since in my first vision quest I was given a Stag heart. So it is highly appropriate that in a journey to the male ancestor, I would meet this creature.

The half-human, half-beast characteristic of this Stag is associated with mythological characters, such as Pan and the Centaur – but with a twist. Pan has the head, chest, and shoulders of a human coupled with the hind end of a goat. The Centaur's top half is human but bottom half is that of a horse. But in my journey the

Stag's bottom half is human, while his top half is beast. In my journey the human half is supplying the regenerative powers of the loins and the motive power of the legs, but the heart and mind are that of a noble beast. I can ask myself what this may say about my concept of the male ancestor.

Another symbol in this journey is that of the horned goddess, of whom *I* was the symbol. The horned goddess of the Etruscan peoples of early Rome was Tana, the goddess of fecundity and fertility. It is interesting that although I knew nothing about Tana until after my journey, when I did some research, the symbolism in my journey is true to her.

It is important to pay attention to recurring aspects in journeys. When you journey you are creating your own mythology, and your own fairy-tale landscape. Here again I am dressed in medieval finery, and medieval symbolism abounds. Since this is a journey to an ancestor, and I am of European descent, the medieval symbolism could be informing me about my actual historical background. Or the medieval symbolism could be present because this era "speaks" to me personally. I resonate with the romance of King Arthur, knights and quests, fair maidens and slaying dragons.

I am aware, of course, that only the nobility of medieval times lived with such pomp and splendor, and in this journey there is also much royal symbolism. Starting with the beginning of the journey, when I notice the bear's back is studded with gemstones, through the ending, when I am feted and cheered by the populace, symbols of queens, goddesses, kings, and consorts, abound. Royalty symbolizes the best of humankind. Since I am the king's consort, I am royal. Through this journey I know that I have the power and the honor and the strength to do what I need to do.

- What symbols did you see in my journey? What universal, cultural or personal meanings do they have for you?

Interpret Your Own Journey

Now it's your turn to interpret your own journey to find a spirit guide. Reread the notes you took after your journey. Ask yourself questions from each perspective. If you can, share your journey with others. Let them give you their interpretations. Listen.

• From the Warrior, who shows up and is ready for action – where did you show up in your journey? What actions did you take?

• From the Teacher, who knows that every story has a lesson and seeks to find it in the journey – where did you notice a lesson in your journey?

• From the Healer, who recognizes that every event has a potential for healing – where did you notice a healing in your journey?

• From the Magician, who translates spiritual insight into practical applications – what is a "real life" application of the insights you received in your journey?

• What are the symbols you noticed in your journey? What universal, cultural, or personal meanings do they have for you?

Aho

Journey to the Female Ancestor

Journeys to the ancestors, both male and female, are good to do when you are experiencing a transition in your life. Perhaps you have graduated from school, or are getting married, or a parent has died, or your children have left home, or you are going through menopause, or you have entered retirement. What's next, you wonder. Ask your ancestors! They have walked these paths before, and have much to show you. They carry the traditions, the stories, and the wisdom of the past.

Journeying to the Female Ancestor helps you understand your inner female, regardless of your gender. You will receive access into her energy and power. Although the feminine has long been denigrated, trivialized, or even demonized in many human cultures, the ancient female archetype is very powerful indeed. She is often venerated as the Mother, or Creator, of All There Is. Your Female Ancestor may help you to become receptive to deep wisdom, and to access your connection to all beings.

Qualities such as nurturance and receptivity may show up in your journey, attributed to you, your guide, or your ancestors. You may experience giving birth, or suckling a child at your breast, or another activity associated with women only. Sometimes your actual relatives, such as a grandmother, aunt, or sister, may appear as your female ancestor in your journey. Or your Female Ancestor may come to you as an animal or a rock or a tree. As you know by now, my female ancestor is an elderly Native American woman I call "Grandmother." However, characteristics generally attributed to the feminine archetype may or may not be what you experience in your journey. This is a personal and intimate interaction.

Let us discover what your female ancestor may have to show you.

Journey to the Female Ancestor

Here is a brief recap of the steps into your journey. A complete explanation of these steps is found in Part One, *How to Journey*.

Step One: Smudge

Place a slow-burning plant material such as cedar or sage in a natural holder such as an abalone shell. Light the material and fan the smoke over you and the room with a feather or your hand. It is the symbolism that is important, so if smoke bothers you do not light the plant material, just pretend to do so.

Step Two: Set Sacred Space

In the space where you are journeying, place seven candles on the floor or on a table. Place one candle in the East, one in the South, one in the West, and one in the North. Place three candles in the middle, one each for Sky Father, Earth Mother, and Creator. Call in the directions as they are outlined in Part One, *How to Journey.*

Take a deep breath.

Step Three: Set Your Intention

Set your intention to visit your Female Ancestor. Say, either aloud or to yourself: "Show me what I need to know about my Female Ancestor."

Step Four: Get Comfortable

Arrange yourself comfortably, either lying or sitting. Nearby have your journey journal, pen and Practical Shamanism mp3 available (go to www.shielabaker.com to get your copy). Cover yourself with a blanket if you wish. Cover your eyes with a scarf, and dim the lights.

Step Five: The Journey

Turn on the Practical Shamanism mp3. Follow the instructions on the mp3. If you do not have this mp3, you may listen to other monotonous sounds such as drums, rattles, or chimes, or simply remain in silence. Then imagine placing yourself in a spirit canoe, and that's a birchbark canoe. On your right-hand side, invite your male ancestors, however they show up: two-legged, four-legged, creepy-crawlers, swimmers, winged ones, the standing people, the trees, the rock nation, or any configuration thereof. On your left-hand side, invite your female ancestors, however they show up. In the stern behind you, place your protection, whatever that is for you. In the bow of your boat, invite your spirit guide. State your intention again. And so it begins. Witness what happens.

Step Six: Record Your Journey

Once you have completed your journey, take a few minutes to write down all that you have experienced. Be as specific as possible. Remember your senses – what did it look like, smell like, sound like, feel like, taste like? Don't worry about punctuation, spelling, or grammar. Don't be judgmental about yourself, your writing ability, or the "quality" of your journey. This is not great literature. You don't need to write the next great novel. Simply tell the story.

Step Seven: Give Thanks

Once again, our female ancestors offered guidance good or not so good and gave us the footing to become who we are. This deserves acknowledgement. Give thanks as it is outlined in Part One, *How to Journey.*

Sharing and Witnessing the Journey

Remember it is a powerful thing to share your journeys with others, and to witness theirs in return. Here is my journey to the Female Ancestor. It has become your journey as well as mine.

Shiela's Journey to the Female Ancestor

On my right is Bear. He has two humps on either side of his head. These humps are new; I have never seen them before. On my left is Grandmother, with many mirror images of her radiating out like a flock of geese heading north. I do not see my guide in the bow of the canoe, or protection in the stern. I actually do not see the canoe at all.

Grandmother steps forward and beckons to me. I step up to her. She pushes me ahead of her, and all the mirror images follow us two by two, in a procession. As the procession marches, I notice that there are animals in line too: wolves, bears, elephants, even bees and ants.

We continue with me leading, although I don't know where I'm going. Suddenly I notice that we form a heart shape. As I notice this I see a hole in the ground. It is too small for me, but I pass into it anyway.

Inside the hole is a downward passageway that opens into a large, well-lit hall. At the far end of this large room is a bed with a canopy. Around the sides of the bed are arranged many women in the shape of butterfly wings. One wing is made up of women of bleeding age, and the other of crones and young girls. On the bed itself, in a place of reverence, is a chrysalis.

Those of us who have come into the room form a heart shape around the chrysalis. I am directly at the anal end. I am to be the midwife.

As the cocoon begins to open, singing and chanting fill the room. I wait but nothing much happens. The opening continues and we wait. We wait some more.

We are waiting, waiting, waiting. The drumbeat softens and we are still waiting. The journey ends.
Aho

Interpreting the Journey

Remember that the following interpretations are mine only, and you are free to agree or disagree with them. You may find meanings in the journey that I do not even mention. Great! Each journey contains many layers, many textures, and many meanings.

From the Warrior, who shows up and is ready for action:

I show up when I answer Grandmother's call to lead. I am willing to step up and lead even when I don't know where we're going.

I show up when I take my place as the midwife at the birthing. I am willing to place myself in a position of power and knowledge.

- Where did you notice me "show up" in my journey?

From the Teacher, who knows that every journey has a lesson:

When I enter the hole that is too small for me, I learn that my ideas of where I fit can be altered. When we judge something to be impossible for us, we often don't even try. But here I learn that the possible depends on angle, perspective, and ultimately, what I think is true. When I pass through the small hole, there is an opening into a large room of light. When I am willing to change my ideas of "fitness," I am rewarded by a new possibility.

Again, waiting is a big lesson in this journey. I must wait for the birth; indeed, the journey actually ends before the birth occurs. This is not easy for me, always anxious for the next step. Some processes cannot be hurried. Transformations, such as fetus into infant or chrysalis into butterfly, have their own time. Even as the midwife, I cannot force or push. I can only wait.

In my journey to the Male Ancestor, the being that I birthed was whisked away before I even knew what her function was. In this journey too, I do not get to see the being that I am helping to be born. The lesson here is non-attachment. When you give birth to a child or a new creative idea, once it is born and out into the world, you have no control. Your work is done, and all you can do is let it go.

• Where did you see a lesson in my journey?

From the Healer, who recognizes that every journey has healing potential:

In this journey I am a midwife, an ancient healer. I join with women of all ages to witness birth and support new life. During most of human history, women helped each other during birth; it is only in recent history that men were allowed into birth chambers. The sacredness of birth is women's ancient domain, bringing all women together. The mirror images radiating from Grandmother in the beginning of the journey reinforce this idea of support as a form of healing.

• Where did you notice a healing in my journey?

From the Magician, who translates insight into application:

Look for images of hearts and butterflies, such as cards or photographs, jewelry, heart-shaped stones, and the like. Use them to decorate a space in your home or office, to remind you of the wisdom of this journey. Do some natural history research. Read about butterflies, or watch a cocoon. Listen to women's birth stories, and tell your own if you have one. Who supported you? How did they do so? Can you pass along this support to someone else?

Ask yourself some soul searching questions suggested by this journey. Where have I been called to lead? Have I been willing to answer this call? Where can I lead now? Where am I trying to push things, instead of waiting for them to happen in their own time?

- Where did you see an action that might be taken from the insights in this journey?

Some symbols and metaphors present in my journey:

This journey is about birth, and symbols of birth are present from the very beginning, when Bear mimics pregnancy with his humps, and Grandmother replicates herself with mirror images. The passageway in the earth is another metaphor for the birth process.

The chrysalis and the butterfly (women in the shape of butterfly wings) symbolize transformation and rebirth in virtually every culture.

The heart shapes in this journey symbolize love and passion. The heart also symbolizes ultimate meaning, as in the heart of the matter.

Finally, the line of animals going two by two is reminiscent of Noah's Ark, where the animals came to be transported and saved.

- What symbols did you see in my journey? What universal, cultural, or personal meanings do they have for you?

Interpret Your Own Journey

Now it's your turn to interpret your own journey to the Female Ancestor. Reread the notes you took after your journey. Ask yourself questions from each perspective. If you can, share your journey with others. Let them give you their interpretations. Listen.

• From the Warrior, who shows up and is ready for action – where did you show up in your journey? What actions did you take?

• From the Teacher, who knows that every story has a lesson and seeks to find it in the journey – where did you notice a lesson in your journey?

• From the Healer, who recognizes that every event has a potential for healing – where did you notice a healing in your journey?

• From the Magician, who translates spiritual insight into practical applications – what is a "real life" application of the insights you received in your journey?

• What are the symbols you noticed in your journey? What universal, cultural, or personal meanings do they have for you?

Aho

Journey to the Warrior

Our next four journeys are to the archetypes of the Warrior, Teacher, Healer, and Magician. The purpose of journeying to these archetypes is to deepen our understanding of these powerful archetypes, and learn how they operate in and illuminate our lives.

The archetype of the Warrior can be confusing. In many people's minds, the Warrior is identified with war, domination, and cruelty. However, this is a narrow, misleading definition. The qualities of a warrior are needed in war, and this is where the word warrior comes from, but the archetype of the Warrior stands independent of war. The dictionary defines warrior as "one who is engaged aggressively or energetically in an activity, cause, or conflict." The Warrior need not be predatory. They need not be armed. A warrior is simply one who takes purposeful action.

A warrior protects his or her tribe or family. A warrior is vigilant: he or she pays attention to their surroundings, alert to clues, hints, or signals about changes in the environment. All their senses are engaged, and ever aware. In my journey classes I describe the Warrior as one who "shows up" or is "fully present." This means the Warrior is the one who steps forward to do what must be done. It means they are focused, not distracted. A warrior is one with a strong intention and the ability to carry through with the intention in the face of danger. A warrior acts in spite of fear. A warrior values the tribe and strategizes, plans and acts for its benefit. Brave, forthright, strong, powerful, tenacious and enduring are some of the adjectives that describe the Warrior. And yes, they can be fierce. They are willing to fight for what they believe and value.

We all have an inner Warrior, who watches out for our best interests, spurs us to stand up for what we believe, and show up for our lives. When we journey to the Warrior, we are accessing this strong, fierce energy. We can learn how to best use it for our good and the good of our particular tribe.

Let us journey to the Warrior archetype and ask to be shown what wisdom or insight the Warrior has for you.

Journey to the Warrior

Here is a brief recap of the steps into your journey. A complete explanation of these steps is found in Part One, *How to Journey.*

Step One: Smudge

Place a slow-burning plant material such as cedar or sage in a natural holder such as an abalone shell. Light the material and fan the smoke over you and the room with a feather or your hand. It is the symbolism that is important, so if smoke bothers you do not light the plant material, just pretend to do so.

Step Two: Set Sacred Space

In the space where you are journeying, place seven candles on the floor or on a table. Place one candle in the East, one in the South, one in the West, and one in the North. Place three candles in the middle, one each for Sky Father, Earth Mother, and Creator.

Call in the directions as they are outlined in Part One, *How to Journey.*

Take a deep breath.

Step Three: Set Your Intention

Set your intention to visit the Warrior. Say, either aloud or to yourself: "Show me what I need to know about the Warrior."

Step Four: Get Comfortable

Arrange yourself comfortably, either lying or sitting. Nearby have your journey journal, pen and Practical Shamanism mp3 available (go to www.shielabaker.com to get your copy). Cover yourself with a blanket if you wish. Cover your eyes with a scarf, and dim the lights.

Step Five: The Journey

Turn on the Practical Shamanism mp3. Follow the instructions on the mp3. If you do not have this mp3, you may listen to other monotonous sounds such as drums, rattles, or chimes, or simply remain in silence. Then imagine placing yourself in a spirit canoe, and that's a birchbark canoe. On your right-hand side, invite your male ancestors, however they show up: two-legged, four-legged, creepy-crawlers, swimmers, winged ones, the standing people, the trees, the rock nation, or any configuration thereof. On your left-hand side, invite your female ancestors, however they show up. In the stern behind you, place your protection, whatever that is for you. In the bow of your boat, invite your spirit guide. State your intention again. And so it begins. Witness what happens.

Step Six: Record Your Journey

Once you have completed your journey, take a few minutes to write down all that you have experienced. Be as specific as possible. Remember your senses – what did it look like, smell like, sound like, feel like, taste like? Don't worry about punctuation, spelling, or grammar. Don't be judgmental about yourself, your writing ability, or the "quality" of your journey. This is not great literature. You don't need to write the next great novel. Simply tell the story.

Step Seven: Give Thanks

Give thanks as it is outlined in Part One, *How to Journey.*

Sharing and Witnessing the Journey

Remember it is a powerful thing to share your journeys with others, and to witness theirs in return. Here is my journey to the Warrior. It has become your journey as well as mine.

Shiela's Journey to the Warrior

Bear comes from my right wearing a black cape, and Grandmother slowly walks in from the left. Her robe has a long train with faces stitched into it. Peacock jumps into the bow of the boat, and behind me is the crystal formation, shimmering. I set my intention to journey to the Warrior to see what there is for me.

I stand in the canoe, arms outstretched. The surface of the water ripples, then becomes turbulent. The boat is rocking. I feel unsteady, so I sit down while the canoe rocks from side to side. I hold onto the sides as the rocking becomes even more turbulent. My knuckles are turning white and I feel slightly queasy. We are still at the shore, not having moved anywhere.

The canoe tips over and is upside down. However, I am still sitting in the canoe, upside down and hanging on. It is so calm under the water. I look up and see that it is choppy on the surface, but here underneath the water it is serene. We are all able to breathe. The canoe rights itself under the water and we travel under the shore bank. It becomes darker as we travel further under the bank. The roots of trees descend very far. We swirl around the roots and go further down. No sunlight reaches here but we can easily see. My hair streams out behind me. It is warm and easy and quiet.

Peacock plays around by fanning his tail out, and seeing how it changes the direction of the canoe. Grandmother is smiling as she rides in her outrigger, and Bear's cape flows behind him. The sense of well-being is very powerful.

I have a sensation of humming in my chest. It accelerates and I feel a cocoon opening at the back of my heart. I am completely held by the water. I feel a lifting in the back of my chest. It feels as though my heart is sprouting wings. I sense they have been there all the time and have just now been released. This image of my winged heart fills me with tremendous power. My body is not used to this sensation, so my mind reacts to it with fear until I wonder, *what if*. What if I just experience this as energy, nothing more or less. I watch as the wings spread. I lift my own arms above my head. The wings fan out and I become the Phoenix. Waves of many feelings wash over me. I am bathed in these feelings and unaware of time. I am like a statue, unmoving, steady, focused, stationary.

I feel this in the core of my being: focused, steady, and immovable. I am sensitive to the water around me, feeling it pass my cheek like the wind on the beach. My wings come down by my side. Once again I am in the canoe with my guides around me, safely back at the point where my journeys always begin. I am home at the shore.

Aho

Interpreting the Journey

Remember that the following interpretations are mine only, and you are free to agree or disagree with them. You may find meanings in the journey that I do not even mention. Great! Each journey contains many layers, many textures, and many meanings.

From the Warrior, who shows up and is ready for action:

I show up by remaining focused and steady, even when I am turned upside down. I maintain my position.

When I wonder *what if,* I conquer my fear and move into wonder instead. I show that I can choose how to perceive what is happening.

I show up in my hyper-awareness of the sensations within my body and the changes in my environment. Extreme awareness is a characteristic of the Warrior.

- Where did you notice me "show up" in my journey?

From the Teacher, who knows that every journey has a lesson:

I learn that turbulence is only present on the surface. The reality underneath the turbulence is serene, calm and quiet. This is good to remember when I am upset.

There is a lesson here about maintaining calm and not giving into panic, when the unforeseen happens. When I take a breath, the canoe rights itself and takes off again. Learning how to manage our breath is a valuable lesson. Breathing promotes calmness so we can see what needs to be done.

Since this is a journey to the Warrior, I am shown, by the humming in my chest and the image of the winged heart, that heart is the basic characteristic of the Warrior.

- Where did you notice a lesson in my journey?

From the Healer, who recognizes that every journey has healing potential:

Water is a great healer, and in this journey I am submerged in it. I am soothed, free, serene, and held completely secure in the embrace of water.

I am healed when I am safely taken home by my guides. My last thought before the journey ends is *I am home at the shore.* There are few concepts as healing as that of home. When we are home we are complete and whole.

- Where did you notice a healing in my journey?

From the Magician, who translates insight into application:

The image of the winged heart is a powerful one. I could draw a heart with a pair of wings sprouting from it, and color it my favorite color. I could frame this image and hang it where I will see it every day.

This journey suggests a longing for water. I could visit a beach, and let the waves wash over me. I could play in the water, and soothe myself by the serenity and timelessness of water.

I could hum, deep in my chest, and place my hand over my heart and feel the vibration of my humming. This way I could feel my heart and my voice acting together.

Soul searching questions I could ask myself include: Where am I immobilized? What kinds of things turn me upside down? How has breathing helped me to survive the turbulence in my life? How can I use my breath to overcome obstacles?

- Where did you notice an action that might be taken from the insights in this journey?

Some symbols and metaphors present in my journey:

The winged heart as a symbol of the Warrior reminds me of Richard the Lion Hearted, or Coeur d'Lion, who was a famous Warrior with a famous heart. The word courage, a characteristic of the warrior, comes from the French word *coeur*, meaning heart.

In this journey I travel through deep roots. I get to the root of the matter, and end up in my own heart – which has wings. The root of the Warrior is heart, but the heart is not stationary. It moves and acts and flies.

- What symbols did you see in my journey? What universal, cultural, or personal meanings do they have for you?

Interpret Your Own Journey

Now it's your turn to interpret your own journey to the Warrior. Reread the notes you took after your journey. Ask yourself questions from each perspective. If you can, share your journey with others. Let them give you their interpretations. Listen.

- From the Warrior, who shows up and is ready for action – where did you show up in your journey? What actions did you take?

- From the Teacher, who knows that every story has a lesson and seeks to find it in the journey – where did you notice a lesson in your journey?

- From the Healer, who recognizes that every event has a potential for healing – where did you notice a healing in your journey?

- From the Magician, who translates spiritual insight into practical applications – what is a "real life" application of the insights you received in your journey?

- What are the symbols you noticed in your journey? What universal, cultural, or personal meanings do they have for you?

Aho

Journey to the Teacher

Today in American society, the teacher has a big job with little reward. "Those who can, do; those who can't, teach," goes the saying. Teachers are not always given the respect they have historically held. Hopefully, this view of teachers is changing, for teaching the young is the most valuable and important role in any civilization.

In ancient societies, the teacher was often the storyteller and the keeper of history. The teacher was the person in the community who held the lessons from the past, without which no person or tribe can grow. They had information and knowledge that others did not have. In addition, their role often required they uphold the standards of morality for the community. Teachers were respected, honored, and obeyed. Their status was high.

When you journey to your internal teacher, you may encounter beings who deserve – and expect – honor, respect, and obedience. You may find yourself in a place of knowledge, such as a classroom, school, or library. Symbols of knowledge, such as books, may be present in your journey.

Each journey has the potential to be a teaching. In meeting your teacher, you are making yourself available to the lessons in each journey. Engaging your teacher will enable you to get the most from your journey experience. You may ask questions relating to daily life and receive answers and instructions. Often these answers or instructions are couched in metaphors that need to be deciphered. This is part of the learning process.

Let us ask what the Teacher has to show you.

Journey to the Teacher

Here is a brief recap of the steps into your journey. A complete explanation of these steps is found in Part One, *How to Journey.*

Step One: Smudge

Place a slow-burning plant material such as cedar or sage in a natural holder such as an abalone shell. Light the material and fan the smoke over you and the room with a feather or your hand. It is the symbolism that is important, so if smoke bothers you do not light the plant material, just pretend to do so.

Step Two: Set Sacred Space

In the space where you are journeying, place seven candles on the floor or on a table. Place one candle in the East, one in the South, one in the West, and one in the North. Place three candles in the middle, one each for Sky Father, Earth Mother, and Creator. Call in the directions as they are outlined in Part One, *How to Journey.*

Take a deep breath.

Step Three: Set Your Intention

Set your intention to visit the Teacher. Say, either aloud or to yourself: "Show me what I need to know about the Teacher."

Step Four: Get Comfortable

Arrange yourself comfortably, either lying or sitting. Nearby have your journey journal, pen and Practical Shamanism mp3 available (go to www.shielabaker.com to get your copy). Cover yourself with a blanket if you wish. Cover your eyes with a scarf, and dim the lights.

Step Five: The Journey

Turn on the Practical Shamanism mp3. Follow the instructions on the mp3. If you do not have this mp3, you may listen to other monotonous sounds such as drums, rattles, or chimes, or simply remain in silence. Then imagine placing yourself in a spirit canoe, and that's a birchbark canoe. On your right-hand side, invite your male ancestors, however they show up: two-legged, four-legged, creepy-crawlers, swimmers, winged ones, the standing people, the trees, the rock nation, or any configuration thereof. On your left-hand side, invite your female ancestors, however they show up. In the stern behind you, place your protection, whatever that is for you. In the bow of your boat, invite your spirit guide. State your intention again. And so it begins. Witness what happens.

Step Six: Record Your Journey

Once you have completed your journey, take a few minutes to write down all that you have experienced. Be as specific as possible. Remember your senses – what did it look like, smell like, sound like, feel like, taste like? Don't worry about punctuation, spelling, or grammar. Don't be judgmental about yourself, your writing ability, or the "quality" of your journey. This is not great literature. You don't need to write the next great novel. Simply tell the story.

Step Seven: Give Thanks

Many of us had Teachers who influenced our lives and gave us the desire to continue our education or find a trade or craft. A long line of Teachers deserve our thankfulness. Give thanks as it is outlined in Part One, *How to Journey.*

Sharing and Witnessing the Journey

Remember it is a powerful thing to share your journeys with others, and to witness theirs in return. Here is my journey to the Teacher. It has become your journey as well as mine.

Shiela's Journey to the Teacher

The Bear comes up to me from my right side. I also notice a Native American man, someone I recognize, standing under a tree on the right side of the shore. On my left is Grandmother, dressed in a halter top and long skirt. Peacock is in the bow and my crystal formation is in the stern of the canoe.

Somehow I travel toward the man standing under the tree, as if I am drawn there across the top of the water. When I reach the tree I am wearing a long fur robe. I am not sure what kind of hide it is made from. The man takes my hand. I am now an old woman. We simply stand there for a few moments, like old friends.

My robe opens and I see that I am naked. A naked old woman. I notice something lying on the ground at my feet. It is a white skin, thin and almost transparent, like a shed snakeskin. I step out of the fur robe, and I am me again, no longer an old woman. A small naked child is hiding behind me.

The man holds out his hand, and the small child comes from behind me and grasps his hand. He thanks me and he and the child, a little girl, turn and walk away. As they do I notice that he has spikes like a dragon down his back. He also has a tail with a spiky spine. The little child has the same.

I watch them walk slowly away as the journey ends.

Aho

Interpreting the Journey

Remember that the following interpretations are mine only, and you are free to agree or disagree with them. You may find meanings in the journey that I do not even mention. Great! Each journey contains many layers, many textures, and many meanings.

From the Warrior, who shows up and is ready for action:

I show up when I recognize the man as an ally, and allow him to take my hand. It is always important to know who your allies are, and who are not.

I show up when I stand for a few minutes and scan the surroundings. Vigilance and protecting one's environment are facets of warrior energy.

- Where did you notice me "show up" in my journey?

From the Teacher, who knows that every journey has a lesson:

Once again I am given a lesson in non-attachment and letting go. I am not attached even to my own skin, or to my age. I shed my skin and step over it. I bring the child, but I am not there to care for her. I let her go. I am not even concerned with the outcome of this journey.

There are different ages represented in this journey: a grown man and a young girl-child, plus my own changing age, from middle age to old, and back again. The lesson here is that age is a superficial attribute that does not affect the central core of who you are.

From the child with the dragon spines, I learn that there may be characteristics, behaviors or even physical attributes that seem to be part of me, but do not belong to me after all. They are merely hiding behind me, and I can safely let them go.

- Where did you see a lesson in my journey?

*From the Healer, who recognizes that every event has
healing potential*:

The acceptance of the aging process in this journey is a profound
healing, especially in our society where youth is more valued than
the wisdom of the aged. Here I recognize that age is just a shift, not
a reality. My acceptance of myself without judgment, seeing
myself naked and old, acknowledges this truth.

Letting go is always healing, and in this journey I let go of much. I
discard my fur robe, and even my own skin, which lies at my feet.
I release the little girl, who represents an underdeveloped piece of
myself I no longer need. I let her go completely; not even curiosity
is present.

- Where did you notice a healing in my journey?

From the Magician, who translates insight into application:

To remind myself of this journey, my actions may include
gathering and displaying a snakeskin, a bit of fur, or a dragon
figure.

Another action would be to ponder some soul searching questions,
such as: What skins am I willing to shed? What piece of myself do
I no longer need? Can I let it go? Are there people in my life now
who could relieve me of these pieces? What are my feelings about
growing old? How do I see my body?

One simple action would be to accept my naked body, especially
where it is starting to show its age. I could stand naked in front of a
mirror and reflect on how beautiful I am.

Skin is an important feature in this journey. An application might
be to take special care of mine.

Have a facial and a massage. Buy some luxurious lotion and smooth it over my skin.

- Where did you see an action that might be taken from the insights in this journey?

Some symbols and metaphors present in my journey:

Although this journey is short, it is rich in symbols. The symbol of the snake is present in the shed skin. The snake is admired by many for this miraculous ability to shed its entire skin and be reborn all at once. Snakeskin is recognized in many cultures as holding powerful medicine. When I shed my skin in this journey (symbolized by the fur robe), it is then that I am able to see things as they really are. I recognize the man and the child as different from me – they are dragon-like creatures.

The dragon is a powerful mythological symbol in cultures the world over. They represent an obstacle to going forward; in many tales the hero must "slay the dragon" before claiming what is his. Dragons are great hoarders, pictured sitting atop a mountain of trinkets, gems, and other glittery things. They don't let go easily. In this journey I am asked to let go of my dragon nature.

When I remove my long, enveloping fur robe, I am reminded of a Native American story of White Buffalo Calf Pipe Woman. In one version of the story, she opened her robe and took a man into her heart, then closed him up with her. When she opened her robe again, the bleached white bones of the man fell down at her feet. They have lived a lifetime of love together.

- What symbols did you see in my journey? What universal, cultural, or personal meanings do they have for you?

Interpret Your Own Journey

Now it's your turn to interpret your own journey to the Teacher. Reread the notes you took after your journey. Ask yourself questions from each perspective. If you can, share your journey with others. Let them give you their interpretations. Listen.

•   From the Warrior, who shows up and is ready for action – where did you show up in your journey? What actions did you take?

•   From the Teacher, who knows that every story has a lesson and seeks to find it in the journey – where did you notice a lesson in your journey?

•   From the Healer, who recognizes that every event has a potential for healing – where did you notice a healing in your journey?

•   From the Magician, who translates spiritual insight into practical applications – what is a "real life" application of the insights you received in your journey?

•   What are the symbols you noticed in your journey? What universal, cultural, or personal meanings do they have for you?

Aho

Journey to the Healer

The word "heal" comes from the old Germanic word *hailaz,* which means "whole." A healer is someone who takes that which is broken or fragmented, and restores it to wholeness. When we are wounded, whether physically, emotionally, mentally, or spiritually, it is an opportunity for us to discover our true selves, in which we are totally complete. When we seek our authenticity, we are seeking our inner healer. We already know how we can heal ourselves, each other, and the Earth herself. This first journey to your healer can bring you a mighty and powerful connection with yourself.

In ancient cultures, healers were not just physicians for the body, but astrologers, wise women, herbalists, midwives, artists, alchemists, singers, dancers, and philosophers. It was recognized that science and religion were not polar opposites, but complementary or even identical. In most societies, healers were revered, respected, and sometimes feared.

Healers are the gatekeepers between life and death. When you were born, a healer likely was there to support your mother and usher you into this world; and when you die, it is probable that a healer will be one of the last faces you see on this earth.

On this journey you may encounter broken things or mended things; beings with wounds, scars, scratches, or cuts; or doctors, nurses, or hospitals. You may be given medicines of some kind, such as pills or herbs; or you may be shown special words to say, chants, or songs. Or maybe none of these things will happen. Remember this is a journey to your own Self, which is completely unique, and completely whole.

Let us journey to discover what the Healer has for you.

Journey to the Healer

Here is a brief recap of the steps into your journey. A complete explanation of these steps is found in Part One, *How to Journey.*

Step One: Smudge

Place a slow-burning plant material such as cedar or sage in a natural holder such as an abalone shell. Light the material and fan the smoke over you and the room with a feather or your hand. It is the symbolism that is important, so if smoke bothers you do not light the plant material, just pretend to do so.

Step Two: Set Sacred Space

In the space where you are journeying, place seven candles on the floor or on a table. Place one candle in the East, one in the South, one in the West, and one in the North. Place three candles in the middle, one each for Sky Father, Earth Mother, and Creator. Call in the directions as they are outlined in Part One, *How to Journey.*

Take a deep breath.

Step Three: Set Your Intention

Set your intention to visit the Healer. Say, either aloud or to yourself: "Show me what I need to know about the Healer."

Step Four: Get Comfortable

Arrange yourself comfortably, either lying or sitting. Nearby have your journey journal, pen and Practical Shamanism mp3 available (go to www.shielabaker.com to get your copy). Cover yourself with a blanket if you wish. Cover your eyes with a scarf, and dim the lights.

Step Five: The Journey

Turn on the Practical Shamanism mp3. Follow the instructions on the mp3. If you do not have this mp3, you may listen to other monotonous sounds such as drums, rattles, or chimes, or simply remain in silence. Then imagine placing yourself in a spirit canoe, and that's a birchbark canoe. On your right-hand side, invite your male ancestors, however they show up: two-legged, four-legged, creepy-crawlers, swimmers, winged ones, the standing people, the trees, the rock nation, or any configuration thereof. On your left-hand side, invite your female ancestors, however they show up. In the stern behind you, place your protection, whatever that is for you. In the bow of your boat, invite your spirit guide. State your intention again. And so it begins. Witness what happens.

Step Six: Record Your Journey

Once you have completed your journey, take a few minutes to write down all that you have experienced. Be as specific as possible. Remember your senses – what did it look like, smell like, sound like, feel like, taste like? Don't worry about punctuation, spelling, or grammar. Don't be judgmental about yourself, your writing ability, or the "quality" of your journey. This is not great literature. You don't need to write the next great novel. Simply tell the story.

Step Seven: Give Thanks

Most of us have had the experience of seeing a healer whether they called themselves midwife, doctor, or shaman or any other name. Some of us owe our lives to these beings. Our loved ones are here because of their training, devotion to their craft and love of life. Give thanks as it is outlined in Part One, *How to Journey.*

Sharing and Witnessing the Journey

Remember it is a powerful thing to share your journeys with others, and to witness theirs in return. Here is my journey to the Healer. It has become your journey as well as mine.

Shiela's Journey to the Healer

I am standing in my canoe. Lightning bolts are in my hands, and I raise my arms. Peacock is clearly illuminated by the upward flying sparks. On my right is Bear, and on my left Grandmother is dancing in a shower of sparks. Behind me my crystals are ablaze in the light. I set my intention to journey to the archetype of the Healer.

We rise above the canyon walls, traveling past a dark spot on the surface of the mesa. We travel over a forest and below I see fires with beings dancing around them. We travel further, around the curve of the Earth, and then jet out toward a bumpy meteor. My hair is flying behind me. Bear and Grandmother are hanging onto the canoe, and Peacock's feet are clamped to the bow. It's as though we're riding on a roller coaster. We are having fun.

We swerve gracefully around planets and other celestial bodies. I am not curious about them. They do not seem important. We are bound beyond the known universe.

Slowing, we come to an orange-colored "something"; my rational senses cannot understand its structure. It is amoeba-like, radiant, glowing. This orange something takes me in and I am embraced by its radiance. I feel warm and begin to relax, my senses still aware but no longer vigilant. This creature, if that is what it is, blankets me with warmth. I feel safe and melt into the fabric of its being. A complete melting occurs and I am literally bathed in the glow of its energy. I acknowledge the energy. I feel my physical heart as a pressure in my chest. I feel not fear, but a sense of oneness and fullness. This pressure moves through my body into my bones and flesh. It remains especially dense around my heart area.

I am now crying. I lie on my side in a fetal position. Something cool strokes my cheek. I am held by warmth but my cheeks are cool; I don't understand. This makes no sense on the physical plane. I am confused but not afraid. My logical mind tells me it is not possible to have confusion without fear.

I stretch out of the fetal position. My body is still warmed and radiated, but I do not feel drained, as I might normally feel after such an emotional release. I just am. I feel the tenderness around my heart, an ache. I feel an ancient blockage there. I ask to have it removed.

I am shown the magic trick of saw blades inserted into a woman's body. The woman is me. The blades in my body are smooth and I feel encouraged to remove them. The orange something opens, and there are my guides: Peacock overhead, Bear and Grandmother on either side, and below my crystal formation. They are not alone; there are many more guides with them. A beheaded Athena comes up to me and bows, offering to help me. Kali is there too, I feel her presence. I ask them to help, and they agree.

My hand goes first to the blade in front, sticking out from my chest. I pull. Athena holds on too, but does not pull. She merely guides as I determine the speed of the removal. When the front blade is out, I feel space between my upper and lower body. I grasp the blade behind me and pull. Kali utters a war cry and I am free of the blades. My body is sore and I feel very tired.

My guides and ancestors pick me up and hold me suspended between them. I spin slowly around while they infuse me with energy and light. My arms lift up from my sides, pointing my hands above my head. I slowly rotate in space, like a roast on a rotisserie. I am baked in radiant light.

Once again I am crying and tears pour off my face. This lasts only a moment, and then I gaze out beyond the perimeter of our small gathering. I see many nebulous things; I am unclear as to what they are. Some are coming closer and others are further away.

I ask to be shown what I must do now. A large shark swims past me. I ask, "Is there more?" I see myself dancing at some gathering. "This is enough," they say, so I thank them.

I move backward through the scene to the fetal position cradled within the orange something. A shaft opens and I slide down the shaft to my canoe. There I sit, wrapped in an orange shawl. The journey ends.

Aho

Interpreting the Journey

Remember that the following interpretations are mine only, and you are free to agree or disagree with them. You may find meanings in the journey that I do not even mention. Great! Each journey contains many layers, many textures, and many meanings.

From the Warrior, who shows up and is ready for action:

I show up right away when I see myself with lightning bolts in my hands. This journey is rich in warrior god symbolism. Zeus, the head of all the gods in the Greek pantheon, holds lightning bolts in his hands. Later, two warrior goddesses, Athena and Kali, show up to help me. They embody fierce and powerful feminine energy.

I show up when I "hang on for dear life" as we are careening through the cosmos, on our celestial roller coaster. I don't scream or cover my eyes; I hang on.

I show up when I ask to have the ancient blockage removed. I willingly undergo an operation, and indeed, do most of the work myself. I also show up when I allow the ancestors to hold me suspended in space. It is the warrior who has the ability to hold, and continue to hold, day after day after day. They don't go home just because it's teatime; they are willing to hold their position for as long as necessary. I show much courage and determination in this journey.

- Where did you notice me "show up" in my journey?

From the Teacher, who knows that every journey has a lesson:

I learn about trust in this journey. When I relax and trust the orange being, I am held and cared for. I learn how to be vulnerable and allow another to care for me.

When I melt into the orange glow, the melting centers around my heart. The lesson is that I must heal my heart first, before I heal anything else. I don't need to understand on an intellectual level. The healing happens deep within the body.

I learn that trust banishes fear. When seeking healing, you need to find help. For instance, if you need an operation, you don't have to become the surgeon yourself in order for the surgery to be successful, or even to understand all the ins and outs of how to conduct the surgery. What you do need is trust in the healer. Trust is an essential component of healing.

The blades that I needed to cut out the blockage were already in my body. I didn't have to go outside myself for the right tools, I already had them. The lesson here is that we already own what we need to heal. We already have the ability to heal ourselves; the tools are given to us, issued with our bodies. Even though we must be willing to accept help from others, the bottom line is that we are the only ones who can heal ourselves.

- Where did you see a lesson in my journey?

From the Healer, who recognizes that every event has healing potential:

I am healed by the orange being, who holds me with love and compassion while I relax and weep. While I am embraced in its glowing warmth, I feel a sense of oneness and completeness.

When I identify the blockage in my heart, I am shown a magic way of healing myself, modeled after a magician's trick of sawing a woman in half. I find the tools I need – the blades – right within my own body, and two powerful female archetypes ready and willing to guide me while I use these tools to cut away what is blocking me from health.

After my operation, my open wound is healed when I am given back to my guides and infused with their energy.

I allow myself to cry copiously in this journey. Tears are our body's healing lubricant, so every time I weep I am contributing to my own heart healing.

- Where did you notice a healing in my journey?

From the Magician, who translates insight into application:

Directions from Spirit are not always wrapped in metaphors; in this journey I am given a clear instruction to obtain an orange shawl for myself. Wrapping myself in this garment will remind me of the healing I did in this journey. In times of mistrust or fear, it will remind me of the love and warmth I found there.

I could examine how I treat myself when I am not feeling well. Do I allow myself to be cared for by others? Do I keep myself warm? Do I feel better if I lay in a fetal position?

Kali utters a war cry in this journey. When there is something that needs healing, or when you need to break free, let out a cry of freedom or triumph. When you are ill, use your voice to get the nasty energy out of yourself. So it would be a good idea for me to create my own healing cry. Or I could try toning or chanting.

- Where did you see an action that might be taken from the insights in this journey?

Some symbols and metaphors present in my journey:

The goddesses Athena and Kali bring meaning profoundly rich in symbolism. Athena is the Greek goddess of wisdom. Kali is the Hindu goddess of destruction and chaos. Both come to help me heal myself.

The fetal position I take symbolizes protection and comfort. When we need a healing, we often regress back to where we were in the ultimate place of protection and caring.

The color orange is prevalent in this journey. Orange represents the second chakra, which corresponds to the regenerative organs of the body and creativity of the mind and spirit. Orange is symbolic of fire, or warmth. It is the color of a tropical fruit, rich in vitamin C, a tool of healing. Finally, orange has a personal meaning for me. Apricot is my favorite color, and my hair is strawberry-blond, which is just a fancy way of saying orange!

- What symbols did you see in my journey? What universal, cultural, or personal meanings do they have for you?

Interpret Your Own Journey

Now it's your turn to interpret your own journey to the Healer. Reread the notes you took after your journey. Ask yourself questions from each perspective. If you can, share your journey with others. Let them give you their interpretations. Listen.

• From the Warrior, who shows up and is ready for action – where did you show up in your journey? What actions did you take?

• From the Teacher, who knows that every story has a lesson and seeks to find it in the journey – where did you notice a lesson in your journey?

• From the Healer, who recognizes that every event has a potential for healing – where did you notice a healing in your journey?

• From the Magician, who translates spiritual insight into practical applications – what is a "real life" application of the insights you received in your journey?

• What are the symbols you noticed in your journey? What universal, cultural, or personal meanings do they have for you?

Aho

Journey to the Magician

The Magician is an alchemist: he or she takes one thing and turns it into another. To our limited senses in our rational framework it seems as though the Magician is bending the rules of reality. This is not so. A Magician has simply learned to manipulate energy.

As I use this archetype, the Magician turns the sometimes paradoxical or even absurd divine guidance into practical applications that can benefit our lives in this world's reality.

In your journey to the Magician, you may be confronted with cultural icons suggesting magic, such as an old man wearing a tall pointy hat, as in the movie *Fantasia.* You may see rabbits being pulled out of hats. You may even run into Doug Henning or David Copperfield doing magic tricks! Or you may not, of course.

Magicians are masters of illusion. Be prepared to see things in a new way in this journey. Look underneath and around what is being shown to you: it may not be what it seems.

Let us journey to discover what the Magician has for you.

Journey to the Magician

Here is a brief recap of the steps into your journey. A complete explanation of these steps is found in Part One, *How to Journey.*

Step One: Smudge

Place a slow-burning plant material such as cedar or sage in a natural holder such as an abalone shell. Light the material and fan the smoke over you and the room with a feather or your hand. It is the symbolism that is important, so if smoke bothers you do not light the plant material, just pretend to do so.

Step Two: Set Sacred Space:

In the space where you are journeying, place seven candles on the floor or on a table. Place one candle in the East, one in the South, one in the West, and one in the North. Place three candles in the middle, one each for Sky Father, Earth Mother, and Creator. Call in the directions as they are outlined in Part One, *How to Journey.*

Take a deep breath.

Step Three: Set Your Intention

Set your intention to visit the Magician. Say, either aloud or to yourself: "Show me what I need to know about the Magician."

Step Four: Get Comfortable

Arrange yourself comfortably, either lying or sitting. Nearby have your journey journal, pen and Practical Shamanism mp3 available (go to www.shielabaker.com to get your copy). Cover yourself with a blanket if you wish. Cover your eyes with a scarf, and dim the lights.

Step Five: The Journey

Turn on the Practical Shamanism mp3. Follow the instructions on the mp3. If you do not have this mp3, you may listen to other monotonous sounds such as drums, rattles, or chimes, or simply remain in silence. Then imagine placing yourself in a spirit canoe, and that's a birchbark canoe. On your right-hand side, invite your male ancestors, however they show up: two-legged, four-legged, creepy-crawlers, swimmers, winged ones, the standing people, the trees, the rock nation, or any configuration thereof. On your left-hand side, invite your female ancestors, however they show up. In the stern behind you, place your protection, whatever that is for you. In the bow of your boat, invite your spirit guide. State your intention again. And so it begins. Witness what happens.

Step Six: Record Your Journey

Once you have completed your journey, take a few minutes to write down all that you have experienced. Be as specific as possible. Remember your senses – what did it look like, smell like, sound like, feel like, taste like? Don't worry about punctuation, spelling, or grammar. Don't be judgmental about yourself, your writing ability, or the "quality" of your journey. This is not great literature. You don't need to write the next great novel. Simply tell the story.

Step Seven: Give Thanks

Give thanks as it is outlined in Part One, *How to Journey.*

Sharing and Witnessing the Journey

Remember it is a powerful thing to share your journeys with others, and to witness theirs in return. Here is my journey to the Magician. It has become your journey as well as mine.

Shiela's Journey to the Magician

I am sitting in my canoe. I call out to my bear who arrives slowly. He is on all fours lumbering toward the far shore. The slowness of his movements brings a sense of calmness over me. As he reaches the water I turn toward the left to look for my female ancestor. Grandmother is sitting under a tree, embroidering a garment. She raises her hand to wave at me.

I face the front of the canoe, where Peacock is perching. I sit patiently waiting and notice the water flowing slowly past. We are not moving. I put my fingers in the water and notice how soft it feels. My back is sore and I breathe into the spot, releasing a pale gray mist around myself. The mist is wet and cool on my skin. No one moves. We are calm and quiet and waiting, waiting.

Ripples begin in front of the boat, and as they hit the bow we are softly bounced away from the shore and out into the current. The ripples become larger and larger, until they lift us off the water and into the air. We are carried on the tip of a wave. The wave flings us out into the air.

I am carried out over the land. Below I watch the fertile land pass beneath me. All is in blossom yet fruit is hanging off every branch of every tree. Golden light bathes us.

I see that I am standing on the edge of a waterfall, and on either side of me are ancestors stretching as far as my eyes can see. Everyone is holding hands. I leap off the waterfall.

Rather than plummeting down, we are lifted up on the air currents and move toward the sun. We are in a V formation like a flock of geese, with me leading. I veer left and we all travel left. I turn my head right and we are taken to the right. I am in charge.

I feel as light as an angel. There is no stress on my arms although we are all linked together. Far below are lakes and valleys and hills. We head toward a body of water. We descend and land as a group on the water. There are so many of us that we cover the entire surface of the lake, bobbing on the surface like a vast group of ducks.

Suddenly we are ducks. We are bobbing on the water. The water underneath my downy belly is cool and filled with fish. There are so many fish that even if we ate all day we could not eat all of them. Some of the ancestors are filling themselves hungrily. I think that it must have been a long time since they nourished themselves because they are gulping and chewing voraciously. But there is more than enough for all.

Many of the ancestors begin gathering together in small groups on the water. They are happy and chatting, and I am smiling. I am glad I've brought them all together. Other ancestors are sleeping with their heads tucked under their wings, some are swimming, and some are diving and splashing in the water like children. Some have their necks entwined, and some are sitting alone, quietly bobbing up and down. I am not drawn to be with any of them. Just gathering them together has been enough for me.

Cherry blossoms drop into the water, landing amidst the ducks. What a beautiful scene, I think; ducks of all kinds with pink blossoms everywhere.

Some of the ducks seem tired and I sense it is now time for them to return. They are very old and unused to this much hubbub. Some have glasses on and are sitting with the younger ducks and telling stories. I can overhear tiny bits of the stories: they are telling the history of our family. I am sad to have to tell them that their time together is over, and I wonder if there is a way for them to stay connected.

Suddenly the water begins to swirl and churn and the ducks are pulled down into a whirlpool that has opened in the middle of the water. The lake becomes a funnel and we all swirl down and down. It is like passing through the constricted part of an hourglass.

Finally out we pop into a grassy field. There are many armchairs in the field and the oldest people are sitting in them. We are all people now, not ducks. I see the armchairs are Lazy Boy recliners and several people are reclining restfully. Several have cups and mugs that hold warm liquid.

The armchairs begin to move around the field as if they were motorized. Some bump into each other, but this just makes the people laugh. Everyone is having fun. There are woods surrounding the field, and from the woods are many eyes watching this scene. I don't know what to make of it so I continue to watch. The sound of laughter is pleasant. The small creatures from the woods – bunnies, foxes, feral cats, and some birds – seem curious and are creeping closer and closer as they watch too.

Now the bumper-car event is over. Each ancestor has an animal close to their chair. The people and the animals are somehow connected. Some ancestors are petting their animal, and some are imitating their calls. All are interacting in some way. There is something significant here that I don't fully understand. Just now I am the watcher.

The ancestors and the animals are to remain here and I am to leave. I feel sad that I must go, but I do. I back away from the scene and find myself at the edge of the waterfall. I am alone this time. I turn around and see my canoe, so I get in and paddle back to the big tree where Grandmother is embroidering the dress. I thank my guides and the journey ends.

Aho

Interpreting the Journey

Remember that the following interpretations are mine only, and you are free to agree or disagree with them. You may find meanings in the journey that I do not even mention. Great! Each journey contains many layers, many textures, and many meanings.

From the Warrior, who shows up and is ready for action:

I show up when I set the direction of my "flock" by turning left or right. I am the leader of the flock and in control.

My job in this journey is to be a watcher. I show up when I pay attention to what is going on in front of me. I do not participate or direct, merely watch.

- Where did you notice me "show up" in my journey?

From the Teacher, who knows that every journey has a lesson:

I learn about the alchemical process; how to make magic. This is a very full journey. One scenario appears, then another, then something shifts, then more things are added. This is a description of the alchemical or experimental process. You have one thing, then you change it a bit, and see what happens. Then you change it some more, and see what happens. You wait for a reaction. When the bumper cars collide, the reaction is laughter. When we swirled down the funnel, we popped out into a field. This is how to bring spirit into matter. You try different things, and some will work.

When I see the ancestors telling the young, and then the animals, the history of my family, I learn that telling ancestral stories connects us to the past, the future, and the natural world itself. Telling our stories allows us to find our place in the world.

I learn that there are no limits in the Magician's realm. Magic takes the ordinary rules of time and space, and goes beyond them.

I learn about leaving. I don't want to leave, but I honor my instinct that tells me it is time to do so.

- Where did you see a lesson in my journey?

From the Healer, who recognizes that every journey has healing potential:

I am healed by the abundance in this journey. There are lots of ducks and even more fish. There are thousands of cherry blossoms. Everyone has a comfortable armchair to rest in. There is freedom and laughter. No one lacks for anything.

This journey is filled with delight. Everyone has a good time, playing games and telling stories. We feast and swim in a flower petaled lake. We ride in bumper cars shaped like armchairs, careening around a field, squealing with laughter. Just to be here makes me feel good.

The connection with the animals is healing. We communicate physically by contact, and emotionally by verbal and psychic communication, bringing understanding between the species.

- Where did you notice a healing in my journey?

From the Magician, who translates insight into application:

I can go have fun! I could seek out a carnival and ride the bumper cars with my friends or family, laughing as we careen harmlessly into each other.

After the fun, I can relax in my own armchair, and if I didn't have a recliner, I might purchase one. I can savor the ease and comfort of this symbol of home.

I could explore my family's stories. If I haven't yet told my story to my own children, I could do so. Or I could seek out my elders and ask them to tell me the stories of our family.

- Where did you see an action that might be taken from the insights in this journey?

Some symbols and metaphors present in my journey:

There is much time symbolism in this journey. In the beginning I notice how slowly the time is passing. I am connected to my ancestors throughout the journey, signifying my connection over time past. We go through a funnel, shaped like an hourglass. Cherry blossoms are symbolic of springtime. The elder ancestors in the journey tell the old stories of our family. The time symbolism reminds me that the Magician is able to manipulate time. In the Magician's realm time is not necessarily what it seems.

The duck is a positive symbol in nearly all cultures. They signify emotional comfort and protection. Since they mate for life, they are symbolic of fidelity and loyalty to their partner and the family. In ancient China, the mandarin duck was symbolic of married bliss. Since ducks can swim, walk, and fly, they are symbolic of resourcefulness and flexibility. Ducks are considered good omens in dreams, signifying that you will be able to elude any difficulty with ease.

The recliners and armchairs symbolize the ease, comfort, and belonging of home. They remind me that life is not supposed to be difficult.

- What symbols did you see in my journey? What universal, cultural, or personal meanings do they have for you?

Interpret Your Own Journey

Now it's your turn to interpret your own journey to the Magician. Reread the notes you took after your journey. Ask yourself questions from each perspective. If you can, share your journey with others. Let them give you their interpretations. Listen.

- From the Warrior, who shows up and is ready for action – where did you show up in your journey? What actions did you take?

- From the Teacher, who knows that every story has a lesson and seeks to find it in the journey – where did you notice a lesson in your journey?

- From the Healer, who recognizes that every event has a potential for healing – where did you notice a healing in your journey?

• From the Magician, who translates spiritual insight into practical applications – what is a "real life" application of the insights you received in your journey?

• What are the symbols you noticed in your journey? What universal, cultural, or personal meanings do they have for you?

Aho

Journey to the Upper World

In the physical realm, we recognize the four cardinal directions of the compass: East, South, West, and North. In the realm of spirit, we also recognize Above, Below, and Center. Our last three journeys will take us to these directions.

The Upper World is also known as Sky Father, or Above. It is associated with illumination and inspiration. This realm is considered the realm of divinity. It is where the light comes from.

The art and science of astrology is based on guidance from above. We look to the stars and the planets to tell us who we are, and where we might be going. In your journey to the Upper World, you may visit the stars, or a particular planet. Clouds may feature in your journeys. You may climb stairs.

A famous Upper World journey is the one Dorothy makes in L. Frank Baum's *The Wizard of Oz*. She travels up in a tornado to a world ruled by a Wizard, the keeper of knowledge. Often when we journey to the Upper World we rise upward in a column of light, or air, or smoke. These paths and many others are all ways to access the Upper World.

Let us journey to the Upper World and ask to be shown what inspiration or illumination it holds for you.

Journey to the Upper World

Here is a brief recap of the steps into your journey. A complete explanation of these steps is found in Part One, *How to Journey*.

Step One: Smudge

Place a slow-burning plant material such as cedar or sage in a natural holder such as an abalone shell. Light the material and fan the smoke over you and the room with a feather or your hand. It is the symbolism that is important, so if smoke bothers you do not light the plant material, just pretend to do so.

Step Two: Set Sacred Space

In the space where you are journeying, place seven candles on the floor or on a table. Place one candle in the East, one in the South, one in the West, and one in the North. Place three candles in the middle, one each for Sky Father, Earth Mother, and Creator. Call in the directions as they are outlined in Part One, *How to Journey.*

Take a deep breath.

Step Three: Set Your Intention

Set your intention to visit the Upper World. Say, either aloud or to yourself: "Show me what I need to know about the Upper World."

Step Four: Get Comfortable

Arrange yourself comfortably, either lying or sitting. Nearby have your journey journal, pen and Practical Shamanism mp3 available (go to www.shielabaker.com to get your copy). Cover yourself with a blanket if you wish. Cover your eyes with a scarf, and dim the lights.

Step Five: The Journey

Turn on the Practical Shamanism mp3. Follow the instructions on the mp3. If you do not have this mp3, you may listen to other monotonous sounds such as drums, rattles, or chimes, or simply remain in silence. Then imagine placing yourself in a spirit canoe, and that's a birchbark canoe. On your right-hand side, invite your male ancestors, however they show up: two-legged, four-legged, creepy-crawlers, swimmers, winged ones, the standing people, the trees, the rock nation, or any configuration thereof. On your left-hand side, invite your female ancestors, however they show up. In the stern behind you, place your protection, whatever that is for you. In the bow of your boat, invite your spirit guide. State your intention again. And so it begins. Witness what happens.

Step Six: Record Your Journey

Once you have completed your journey, take a few minutes to write down all that you have experienced. Be as specific as possible. Remember your senses – what did it look like, smell like, sound like, feel like, taste like? Don't worry about punctuation, spelling, or grammar. Don't be judgmental about yourself, your writing ability, or the "quality" of your journey. This is not great literature. You don't need to write the next great novel. Simply tell the story.

Step Seven: Give Thanks

Give thanks as it is outlined in Part One, *How to Journey.*

Sharing and Witnessing the Journey

Remember it is a powerful thing to share your journeys with others, and to witness theirs in return. Here is my journey to the Upper World. It has become your journey as well as mine.

Shiela's Journey to the Upper World

I stand in my canoe taking deep breaths. I am shaking off the day; I need this because I am a two-legged with constraints from the physical plane. Inhaling, I release all that does not serve me here. I settle. Suddenly Bear on my right does a belly flop, splashing me. So much for taking things seriously! Turning left I see Grandmother leaning against a tree. She smiles like a tolerant auntie watching children play. Peacock is less tolerant and huffing a bit. "Come on, let's go! I have much to show you," he says. In the back are my crystals. I set my intention to journey to the Upper World.

I notice that I am dressed in a luminescent robe, white, long, and flowing with big billowy sleeves. I stretch out my arms and feel a sudden sense of lightness.

I become aware of a spot on my back, which I often feel on the physical plane. It hums under my left shoulder blade. Physically there is a lot going on with my body, tightness here, humming there. It irritates me slightly, but I just notice. I take another deep releasing breath and I imagine myself at peace. I am aware of the inside of my nostrils; how the air passes up the back of my nose, curves and flows down my throat.

I feel like making this experience upside down, and it is. The canoe becomes the curve of the new moon, just a few days old. I am hanging upside down bathed in moonlight. My smile is like the moon and it stretches my face. I wonder what this is. Whoops, I'm right side up! But I'm still in the moon. Now I am the Man in the Moon! I reach out my arms and touch the perimeter of the moon. The moon is like the head of a drum with me painted on its face. Suddenly I am hanging over a soft and fragrant mushroom. My cheek rests on the mushroom cap. It feels furry. I look around and see that the mushroom is not growing in earth but is suspended in space.

Moving over I hang from the edge of the mushroom. I let go and fall. There are white rootlike tentacles that I grab onto because there is nothing else below me, nothing! I climb up the tentacles and enter the stem of the mushroom. I travel up inside the stem and emerge through the pores of the cap. I look around and see there are several of me. This freaks me out. I want to be all together.

I notice that the mushroom is no longer. Now I am climbing a white marble statue of a woman, like those you see in churches. All the little *me*s climb up and slide down the robes of this statue.

Suddenly, as if on cue, the little *me*s run and hide in the robes of the woman. We are all very still. The statue has another robe I had not noticed, and she pulls that about her. We are plunged into darkness.

It is warm in the darkness. I am tired. I look up and see only darkness where the face of the statue should be. I feel no fear, only warm and comfortable and relaxed. Cool white marble enveloped in dark warm comfort. We all float off into dreamtime.

I am now an observer from outside this scene, and I see us moving toward a place where there are several dark, cloaked shapes like the one we are traveling in. They form a circle, reminding me of the Knights of the Round Table. We are brought out from under the cloak all white and glowing.

We emerge out of the white robes. We are a toadstool with squidlike arms coming out the bottom. We are special, a new thing entirely. No one else has anything that looks like us. We are examined while oohs and aahs surround us. Aren't we grand? Everyone gets a "hold the new thing" time, as we are passed around and admired.

Without warning we are bashed against the hard tabletop and shattered. Disoriented and dizzy, we wander around the statue that has been broken, although we are not. There are several of us still, and we come together in a huddle. We aren't frightened, just stunned.

Each of the black-cloaked beings – a wraith I think – takes one of the *me*s. As I am taken the wraith lets out a great howl. I am carried within the warm robes, comfortable and relaxed. I am riding inside a tiny red envelope tucked where the heart would be.

Ceremonial greetings and partings are going on and I realize that I am not to be reunited with the other *me*s at this time. I have no fear, only knowing. We all move away from the table. The journey ends.

Aho

Interpreting the Journey

Remember that the following interpretations are mine only, and you are free to agree or disagree with them. You may find meanings in the journey that I do not even mention. Great! Each journey contains many layers, many textures, and many meanings.

From the Warrior, who shows up and is ready for action:

I show up by "shaking off" the day and bring myself present for the journey. I am making sure I am ready for whatever comes.

There is much frenetic energy present in this journey – a lot happens in a jumble. My warrior aspect keeps track of what is happening. I track all the little *me*s as they scurry around climbing and sliding. They are an active little group, but I am the shepherd who knows where they all are at all times.

- Where did you notice me "show up" in my journey?

From the Teacher, who knows that every journey has a lesson:

As soon as I feel like making the experience upside down, reality shifts to accommodate my thoughts. I learn here that I create my own reality. This is a profound lesson in the power of our own thoughts.

I break apart and remain in separate pieces throughout the experience. I do not reassemble into a whole. I do not have to put the pieces back together. Although at first I am "freaked out" by this experience, later I am not afraid. Instead, I feel warmth and comfort. I learn that if fear is not perceived, it does not exist. Again, I am creating my own reality – in this case, the reality of my emotions.

- Where did you see a lesson in my journey?

From the Healer, who recognizes that every event has healing potential:

I am healed when I hide inside the cloak of the white marble woman. The darkness is so warm and comfortable that I float off into dreamtime. I am healed by the darkness itself. This is symbolic of our mother's womb, a place where we lived before we were wounded or separated.

I am healed when I realize how unique and special I am – a new thing entirely. I allow myself to be admired. I listen to the oohs and aahs of admiration and know that I am grand.

A healing occurs when I become the heart of a black wraith. Although this could be a scary image, reminiscent of something out of *Lord of the Rings*, I am comfortable and relaxed. It does not bother me that I am not to be reunited with the other *me*s. I am needed where I am.

- Where did you notice a healing in my journey?

From the Magician, who translates insight into application:

Ways to concretize this journey might include wearing a white cloak or a black one. I could acquire an inexpensive statue of a white woman, and then smash it. I could pick some mushrooms (but not eat them!).

I could let myself accept compliments and receive admiration, without false modesty, disclaimers, or egotism. I could even ask for compliments, so I could practice this skill. Acknowledging our own beauty and uniqueness can be uncomfortable. In our culture, we are not usually taught to graciously receive admiration. I know I would like to be better at this.

Because mushrooms are a feature of this journey, I could pay attention to the beauty and uniqueness of this wonderful fungus. I could serve mushrooms for dinner. At the proper season, I could go on a "mushroom walk," taking photographs of the mushrooms I find growing in the fields, woods, and neighborhood lawns. (In the Pacific Northwest where I live, mushrooms are wildly prolific in the autumn.)

Finally, I could ask myself some soul searching questions. This journey is concerned with fragmentation and wholeness, seeming to suggest that we are both fragmented and whole at the same time. Where in my life do I feel fragmented? Do I feel that I have pieces "missing"? Am I conscious of more than one "me"?

- Where did you see an action that might be taken from the insights in my journey?

Some symbols and metaphors present in my journey:

This is a journey to the Upper World, so it is not surprising there are symbols of this realm present. The jumbled, shifting energy reminds me of the galaxies that are continually forming. They are constantly making "new things entirely." The night sky might look calm to us here on earth, but in reality it is filled with shifting, pulsing, shimmering energy. It is broken into a zillion pieces at all times, breaking apart and coming together.

The moon, another Upper World symbol, represents mystery in many cultures. In this journey it is specifically the new moon, which symbolizes rebirth, as does the Upper World itself.

Mushrooms are a symbol for transformation into alternate realities, as in Lewis Carroll's *Alice in Wonderland*. Some mushrooms in this reality have mind-altering properties. Mushrooms are also a symbol for the death/rebirth cycle, as they often sprout in decaying matter.

The color symbolism of this journey juxtaposes white and black. There are beings in white robes, representing purity, and other beings in black robes, representing mystery and death in the form of wraiths.

The red envelope that is tucked into the heart space of a wraith reminds me of feng shui envelopes, which are meant to hold money symbolizing abundance. In this journey the money is put where the heart is.

- What symbols did you see in my journey? What universal, cultural, or personal meanings do they have for you?

Interpret Your Own Journey

Now it's your turn to interpret your own journey to the Upper World. Reread the notes you took after your journey. Ask yourself questions from each perspective. If you can, share your journey with others. Let them give you their interpretations. Listen.

From the Warrior, who shows up and is ready for action – where did you show up in your journey? What actions did you take?

From the Teacher, who knows that every story has a lesson and seeks to find it in the journey – where did you notice a lesson in your journey?

From the Healer, who recognizes that every event has a potential for healing – where did you notice a healing in your journey?

From the Magician, who translates spiritual insight into practical applications – what is a "real life" application of the insights you received in your journey?

What are the symbols you noticed in your journey? What universal, cultural, or personal meanings do they have for you?
Aho

Journey to the Lower World

The Lower World is the realm of the unconscious, the land of shadows. It is where we keep things from ourselves that we do not wish to know, or that we fear. In some cultures and eras it was thought that this land was best kept "under" wraps.

In journeying to the Lower World we begin to bring thoughts, ideas, and actions from this realm into light and consciousness. Many great ideas have been lying dormant here. This is where we find our beliefs about our own limitations and what has been holding us back. Because they have been unseen and unacknowledged, we have been unable to act upon them.

Often access to the Lower World is achieved by descent through tunnels, caves, tree roots or many other "downward" paths. A famous Lower World journey can be found in Lewis Carroll's *Alice in Wonderland* where Alice descends into the Lower World via a rabbit hole.

In your journey to the Lower World, you may meet beings who live underground, such as moles, groundhogs, or worms. You may find yourself in cellars or basements, or under bridges or inside tunnels. It may be dark or murky in the Lower World. You may travel under water, or into caves or hidden subterranean passageways.

Let us journey to the Lower World and ask to be shown what it may hold for you.

Journey to the Lower World

Here is a brief recap of the steps into your journey. A complete explanation of these steps is found in Part One, *How to Journey.*

Step One: Smudge

Place a slow-burning plant material such as cedar or sage in a natural holder such as an abalone shell. Light the material and fan the smoke over you and the room with a feather or your hand. It is the symbolism that is important, so if smoke bothers you do not light the plant material, just pretend to do so.

Step Two: Set Sacred Space

In the space where you are journeying, place seven candles on the floor or on a table. Place one candle in the East, one in the South, one in the West, and one in the North. Place three candles in the middle, one each for Sky Father, Earth Mother, and Creator. Call in the directions as they are outlined in Part One, *How to Journey.*

Take a deep breath.

Step Three: Set Your Intention

Set your intention to visit the Lower World. Say, either aloud or to yourself: "Show me what I need to know about the Lower World."

Step Four: Get Comfortable

Arrange yourself comfortably, either lying or sitting. Nearby have your journey journal, pen and Practical Shamanism mp3 available (go to www.shielabaker.com to get your copy). Cover yourself with a blanket if you wish. Cover your eyes with a scarf, and dim the lights.

Step Five: The Journey

Turn on the Practical Shamanism mp3. Follow the instructions on the mp3. If you do not have this mp3, you may listen to other monotonous sounds such as drums, rattles, or chimes, or simply remain in silence. Then imagine placing yourself in a spirit canoe, and that's a birchbark canoe. On your right-hand side, invite your male ancestors, however they show up: two-legged, four-legged, creepy-crawlers, swimmers, winged ones, the standing people, the trees, the rock nation, or any configuration thereof. On your left-hand side, invite your female ancestors, however they show up. In the stern behind you, place your protection, whatever that is for you. In the bow of your boat, invite your spirit guide. State your intention again. And so it begins. Witness what happens.

Step Six: Record Your Journey

Once you have completed your journey, take a few minutes to write down all that you have experienced. Be as specific as possible. Remember your senses – what did it look like, smell like, sound like, feel like, taste like? Don't worry about punctuation, spelling, or grammar. Don't be judgmental about yourself, your writing ability, or the "quality" of your journey. This is not great literature. You don't need to write the next great novel. Simply tell the story.

Step Seven: Give Thanks

Give thanks as it is outlined in Part One, *How to Journey*.

Sharing and Witnessing the Journey

Remember it is a powerful thing to share your journeys with others, and to witness theirs in return. Here is my journey to the Lower World. It has become your journey as well as mine.

Shiela's Journey to the Lower World

On my right is Bear sitting under a tree. His belly is distended and he is happily licking his fingers. On my left Grandmother is standing with her hands on hips, shaking her head and chuckling. "I told him, don't eat so much," she says. Peacock excitedly calls,

"Get in the canoe, let's go! I have much to show you." The canoe has red velvet seats. My crystals are in the stern as usual. I say, "I want to go the Lower World, please."

Off we go. Spinning wildly, we descend down a whirlwind in the water. I can see only the silver sides of the water tunnel. It is a long tunnel and I am having fun, as if I am at an amusement park. We fly out the end of the tunnel into wide-open space. "It's a good thing I don't have any expectations," I think. The open space is very bright; gold speckles twinkle in the air, as if the atmosphere were made of gold confetti.

A huge Viking-style boat is heading straight toward us. There is a fiery lion at the bow, but I see no one else on deck. Big oars extend out from the sides of the ship. The oars dip deep into the water and bring up seaweed, dark and dank. The slippery seaweed hangs from the oars.

A door opens in the Viking boat, inviting me to a cabin below. Naturally, I accept and enter. It's warm and beautiful in the cabin. Crystal and candles light up a sumptuous repast on the table. It smells divine and I am curious. Looking around I see no one. My attire has changed. I am cinched into a corseted gown, my hair is atop my head and I am wearing large dangly earrings. I feel beckoned to the table.

I sit at the table and sip golden liquid out of a crystal goblet. Beginning to relax, I take a breath.

Sweet soft music fills the room. I forget that I am on an abandoned ship somewhere. I notice that I feel woozy, a little furry around the edges. "I am warm and woozy," I think, and giggle.

The room seems to fill up but I can see no one. But I do feel a presence, or many presences. On some level I am engaged in several conversations at once. My head reels.

My body reels too; spinning, I feel my clothes fly off my body. Now I am bare and in a jungle. I am still warm and woozy, but now I am running. I am running through the jungle, away from something. I hear panting behind me and I run faster. I don't dare look behind me. Adrenaline is pumping through my veins. Running, running, running. Nowhere to turn. Leaves brush my body, damp with jungle dew.

Even though I have been running for a long time, I am not tired. I look down at my body and instead of my arms, I see the legs of a black cat. I am a panther. My energy is not mine anymore, but that of this animal. I keep on going, still not daring to look behind me. I bound farther and farther.

Now I am on a Savannah, with a herd of other animals. They don't seem to notice me, and I slink under the belly of an elephant. Panting, I feel the bulk of his belly on my back. I glance around but I sense nothing; the herds of animals are content.

I wait. Elephant picks up his foot and gives my butt a boot. I creep out toward the water hole. Looking in the water I see myself. I stand up and shake, for I see that I am a two-legged again! I feel dazed.

I assess the situation. I am on a savannah. My guides are not around. Herds of wild animals surround me. I am unarmed. What does this mean? I call out, "AAAHHHOOO! AAAHHHOOO!" A primitive cry to my ancestors.

From behind the bushes, trees, and small shrubs dotting the savannah, small people caked in dried earth come toward me. They laugh at me, for I am naked and not protected from the sun. With utmost care and true affection they pack mud on me. Now I am protected.

Someone plays a welcoming song on a wood flute. The animals continue to graze and act as if we do not exist. The sun sets and I am taken home by the mud people. I am aware that their home is where I begin my journeys each time: at the edge of my river, but when times were not as they are now. I am home and so are they. The journey ends.

Aho

Interpreting the Journey

Remember that the following interpretations are mine only, and you are free to agree or disagree with them. You may find meanings in the journey that I do not even mention. Great! Each journey contains many layers, many textures, and many meanings.

From the Warrior, who shows up and is ready for action:

I show up when I acknowledge that I have no expectations for this journey, but am alert for whatever comes.

I show up when I go aboard the Viking ship, a symbol of Warrior energy, as the Vikings were known as great warriors. I readily accept the invitation I am given to enter this realm, showing bravery.

I show up when I become the panther, a creature known for its stealth, cunning and swiftness, all attributes of the Warrior.

Lastly, I show up when I find myself alone and unarmed on the savannah, and give voice to a great war cry that calls to my tribe.

- Where did you notice me "show up" in my journey?

From the Teacher, who knows that every journey has a lesson:

I am taught about adaptability and flexibility in this journey. I shape shift from a two-legged to a panther and back again. I travel from a ship at sea, to a jungle, to a savannah, and everywhere I go I try to find a way to fit in with my surroundings. When I am invited to enter the surroundings on the Viking boat, I am given food and drink and warm surroundings. When I charge into the jungle, I am enveloped in fear. When I ask for help on the savannah by calling for my ancestors, I am welcomed. These different experiences teach me how to be a good guest.

The elephant teaches me that stealth and cunning does not always serve me. When I am trying to hide underneath the elephant, it kicks me in the butt. This motivates me to give myself a shake, and I regain my humanity.

When the mud people find me naked and unprotected on the savannah, they laugh at me, but with affection. This teaches me to take life lightly and laugh at myself.

- Where did you see a lesson in my journey?

From the Healer who recognizes that every event has healing potential:

Elephant heals me by giving me a swift kick in the rear. I am jolted into seeing who I am really am. When I do my fear dissipates.

I am healed when my ancestors the mud people respond to my call. They treat me with true affection and play a welcoming song for me on wooden flutes. They cover me with mud, both to protect me from the hot sun and to welcome me into their tribe. I am the guest who becomes family. Indeed, at the end of the journey I see that their home and mine are the same. Coming home is always healing.

- Where did you notice a healing in my journey?

From the Magician, who translates insight into application:

This journey deals much with welcoming and visiting. Therefore a good action would be to have visitors in my home, or go visiting myself. It would be a good idea to accept any invitations I receive now, and allow myself to feel welcome. Similarly, I could issue invitations myself, and pay attention to making my guests feel welcome and at home.

There is a lot of spinning and twirling in this journey, usually right before a change. As a fun experiment, I could spin around in my living room, and see how my perception changes.

The experience with the elephant might motivate me to ask myself some questions, such as: How do I try to hide? Do I run away when frightened? Who kicks me in the butt when I am trying to hide? How can I find a helpful elephant?

An action suggested by this journey would be to use my voice. I could create my own "war cry" and shout it with all my being, calling for my ancestors. I could also create or discover my "welcome home" song, and sing or play it for myself.

- Where did you see an action that might be taken from the insights in this journey?

Some symbols and metaphors present in this journey:

To me, the Lower World is about paring down and moving backward in time, to an ancient, more primitive past closely aligned with the earth. I go back in time to the Viking era, then back even further to the primitive mud people.

In the Viking ship, there are golden speckles in the air, and I drink a golden drink that opens into the next stage of the adventure. Gold symbolizes spiritual purity.

Again in this journey my attire is a major symbol. First I am dressed in an elegant gown with a corset and wear an elaborate hairdo, symbolizing wealth and luxury. But when next I am human I am completely naked, being burned by the sun. This reminds me of the ancient story of Inanna and Erishkegal, in which Inanna goes through the seven gates and loses all of her clothing, ending up completely naked.

There are two animal symbols in this journey, the black panther and the elephant. The panther represents buried truth in the underworld; the ability to know the dark. Panthers move gracefully but stealthily, and are celebrated for their cunning. Elephants symbolize strength and royalty; and also, confidence, patience, and wisdom. In this journey the elephant is shown to be wiser than the panther.

- What symbols did you see in my journey? What universal, cultural, or personal meanings do they have for you?

Interpret Your Own Journey

Now it's your turn to interpret your own journey to the Lower World. Reread the notes you took after your journey. Ask yourself questions from each perspective. If you can, share your journey with others. Let them give you their interpretations. Listen.

- From the Warrior, who shows up and is ready for action – where did you show up in your journey? What actions did you take?

- From the Teacher, who knows that every story has a lesson and seeks to find it in the journey – where did you notice a lesson in your journey?

• From the Healer, who recognizes that every event has a potential for healing – where did you notice a healing in your journey?

• From the Magician, who translates spiritual insight into practical applications – what is a "real life" application of the insights you received in your journey?

• What are the symbols you noticed in your journey? What universal, cultural, or personal meanings do they have for you?

Aho

Journey to the Center

The Native American elder, Black Elk, said, "The center of the world is where you are." When we journey to the center, we journey to the core of ourselves.

Having journeyed thirteen times, you now have a deep knowing about how to journey. Your core is the center of deep knowing, the place where you know the truth of all. Journeying to the center is sometimes like journeying to Creator, the Great Spirit, All That Is, God, the Great Mystery, or simply the One. Because of this, the center is very difficult to describe. It is whatever it is for you.

Journey into the Center now and ask to be shown what it has for you.

Journey to the Center

Here is a brief recap of the steps into your journey. A complete explanation of these steps is found in Part One, *How to Journey.*

Step One: Smudge

Place a slow-burning plant material such as cedar or sage in a natural holder such as an abalone shell. Light the material and fan the smoke over you and the room with a feather or your hand. It is the symbolism that is important, so if smoke bothers you do not light the plant material, just pretend to do so.

Step Two: Set Sacred Space

In the space where you are journeying, place seven candles on the floor or on a table. Place one candle in the East, one in the South, one in the West, and one in the North. Place three candles in the middle, one each for Sky Father, Earth Mother, and Creator. Call in the directions as they are outlined in Part One, *How to Journey.*

Take a deep breath.

Step Three: Set Your Intention

Set your intention to visit the Center. Say, either aloud or to yourself: "Show me what I need to know about the Center."

Step Four: Get Comfortable

Arrange yourself comfortably, either lying or sitting. Nearby have your journey journal, pen and Practical Shamanism mp3 available (go to www.shielabaker.com to get your copy). Cover yourself with a blanket if you wish. Cover your eyes with a scarf, and dim the lights.

Step Five: The Journey

Turn on the Practical Shamanism mp3. Follow the instructions on the mp3. If you do not have this mp3, you may listen to other monotonous sounds such as drums, rattles, or chimes, or simply remain in silence. Then imagine placing yourself in a spirit canoe, and that's a birchbark canoe. On your right-hand side, invite your male ancestors, however they show up: two-legged, four-legged, creepy-crawlers, swimmers, winged ones, the standing people, the trees, the rock nation, or any configuration thereof. On your left-hand side, invite your female ancestors, however they show up. In the stern behind you, place your protection, whatever that is for you. In the bow of your boat, invite your spirit guide. State your intention again. And so it begins. Witness what happens.

Step Six: Record Your Journey

Once you have completed your journey, take a few minutes to write down all that you have experienced. Be as specific as possible. Remember your senses – what did it look like, smell like, sound like, feel like, taste like? Don't worry about punctuation, spelling, or grammar. Don't be judgmental about yourself, your writing ability, or the "quality" of your journey. This is not great literature. You don't need to write the next great novel. Simply tell the story.

Step Seven: Give Thanks

Give thanks as it is outlined in Part One, *How to Journey.*

Sharing and Witnessing the Journey

Remember it is a powerful thing to share your journeys with others, and to witness theirs in return. Here is my journey to the Center. It has become your journey as well as mine.

Shiela's Journey to the Center

I stand in my canoe, arms outstretched. Bear swims across the stream to greet me. Grandmother is sitting at the edge of the water in the shade of a big tree. Peacock stretches his tail feathers, mimicking me. Behind me is my crystal formation. I set my intention to journey to the Center.

The canoe spins around a few times. I am caught off-guard, and I wobble, laughing. The canoe bumps gently on the sandy shore. I get out of the boat and walk along the shore. I am searching for something. A solitary boulder sits on the beach. I climb and sit atop the warm rock. I lie back and soak up the warmth, my body fully supported by the boulder. I smile and stretch out, relaxing. I watch my guides playing together.

I feel a tingling in my gut. Nothing seems amiss, yet I am alert. My guides are quiet. I become even more alert, waiting and watching. I feel anticipation. The wind stills. I sit up on the rock, ever more vigilant. The anticipation is exciting yet nerve-racking at the same time.

In the distance I see something that I can't quite make out. It looks like specks, many of them coming toward me. My guides come out of the water and move toward me. They gather around me. We wait together. The wind and water are quiet. No birds sing.

Anticipation is heavy in the air. My heart beats faster. I wonder where my drum is – how could I have left her behind? Suddenly my drum appears, and I drum softly, just waiting. The specks are getting bigger. They are still a long way off, way down the beach. With my drum in hand, I feel less anxious, more in charge. I pick up the beat and call out to whatever is coming.

My guides gather around the rock, moving to the beat of my drum. I feel secure because I know they can take care of me. The specks continue to approach, moving in slow motion. I discover that changing the rhythm of the drum changes nothing. I continue to drum and wait. I have no effect upon the course of events. The specks still move slowly toward me. I am mesmerized by my own drumbeat and lose interest in the specks. I am in my own world.

I stand and sway to my own rhythm. Occasionally I glance down the beach. The specks are taking their own sweet time. I become curious again. Nothing I have done has had an effect on the specks. What is this? I know I am the creator of my world, that I affect everything in my life. So why not this?

The specks are now close enough to see. They appear to be round dark balls, each with a red dot in the center and other markings around the circumference. The largest ball begins to separate in the middle. It comes apart. Its core is a stick, holding the two halves apart. The stick has tentacles that reach out beyond the edge of the ball. They are searching for something.

Wiggling this way and that, the tentacles reach out and take some sand into the ball. Now there are three other balls doing the same thing, also discovering. We watch. The balls don't seem to sense our presence. I sneeze, and this causes the balls to close quickly.

Slowly the balls open again, and I begin to drum softly. My guides and I do not feel threatened, only curious.

The balls huddle together and a red dot pulses. The red dot is directed at my male ancestor, Bear. Bear sits down and a small ball comes rolling to him. I become nervous and drum again, because drumming quells my nervousness. Bear and the ball are somehow communicating. Bear touches the ball, and his big paws have a luminescent dust on them. He tastes the dust and gives a contented grunt. I smile because I have heard his grunt of pleasure before. Still, I am nervous. Another ball rolls over to Grandmother. She touches it, smiles, and then laughs. Peacock lands on my shoulder, calming me.

I get down from the boulder. I think, "Well, there must be something for me!" A ball rolls to me. I am engulfed in a wonderful aroma very much to my liking. I smile. "But...." I think, "What about the biggest ball? Why is that not for me?"

The balls regroup. We watch as they slowly roll back down the beach. I stretch out again on the rock. My guides go back to playing in the water. It looks the same as before. I wonder and question, "Did this really happen? What does it mean?"

I notice a small white flower tucked behind Grandmother's ear. Bear has a neckerchief that was not there before. I am curious – what is different about me? I ask my guides this question. I am told that I have a mark on my forehead. So I have been marked, but for what?

I thank my guides for witnessing this and they bow. We head back to the canoe and prepare to return to the mundane world. The drumbeat softens and we are back by the edge of the water where we always begin our journey.

Aho

Interpreting the Journey

Remember that the following interpretations are mine only, and you are free to agree or disagree with them. You may find meanings in the journey that I do not even mention. Great! Each journey contains many layers, many textures, and many meanings.

From the Warrior, who shows up and is ready for action:

I show up after I am caught off guard. I have a tingling in my gut, and I am fully alert, waiting and watching for whatever comes. All my senses are engaged, and I am determined not to be caught off guard again.

I show up when I calm myself by drumming. When I notice that I am nervous, I do something that makes me feel less so. It is my responsibility to take care of my emotional states in order to manage my own fears.

- Where did you notice me "show up" in my journey?

From the Teacher, who knows that every journey has a lesson:

Although this is a journey to the Center, one of the lessons I learn is that I am not always the center! It's not all about me. I have little effect upon the balls. When I try to control them, they remain the same; but when I sneeze, an involuntary action outside my control, they do show an effect. Also, I am only one of the players in this journey; the balls come to all of us, and I don't even get the biggest one!

I learn non-attachment. My ancestors are not attached to having the balls, in contrast to me. I want a ball for myself, and not just any ball, but the biggest ball. My ancestors are left with remembrances, a white flower and a neckerchief, but these can be taken off. My remembrance, on the other hand, is permanent, a brand on my skin.

My desire for the "best" or biggest ball has marked me, while my ancestors' non-attachment has left them free.

- Where did you see a lesson in my journey?

From the Healer, who recognizes that every journey has healing potential:

I am healed by my own drumming. My nervousness and fear is replaced by calm. Music has always been acknowledged as a great healer.

Play is also a known healer, and this journey contains much play. My ancestors enjoy playing with the balls. The balls give much sensory pleasure: the luminescent dust from the ball tastes good to Bear, and Grandmother enjoys touching her ball. The ball I am given to play with has a wonderful scent, although I do not enjoy my ball as much as my ancestors, because I am distracted by greed and jealousy.

I am given healing when Peacock lands on my shoulder. I am reminded that simple touching, body to body, can heal us.

- Where did you notice a healing in my journey?

From the Magician, who translates insight into application:

An action I can and do take is to drum when I am uncertain. This always has a quieting effect on me.

I could ask myself if I always need to have the biggest or the best. Can I let someone else have the biggest? Can I be content with what I am given? I might practice taking the smallest portion of something.

I could give myself time to play! I might even play ball or another "children's" game, enjoying all the sights, sounds, tastes, and scents of the play experience.

- Where did you notice an action that might be taken from the insights in this journey?

Some symbols and metaphors present in my journey:

There are several symbols and metaphors for Center in this journey. Nearly the first thing that happens is that I am knocked "off-center." The center is often symbolized by a round shape such as an orb or ball. The small balls with their dots (another round shape) symbolize pieces of my center. They symbolize atoms or molecules, from the center of all beings.

The balls are searching for something, and the largest ball has tentacles. This reminds me of a probe from outer space, investigating our world.

At the end of the journey, we are all changed. Bear has a neckerchief, Grandmother has a flower, and I have a mark on my head. The balls, too, are marked with a red dot. We have all been marked for, or by, something. Perhaps by God, or perhaps by our own faith.

- What symbols did you see in my journey? What universal, cultural, or personal meanings do they have for you?

Interpret Your Own Journey

Now it's your turn to interpret your own journey to the Center. Reread the notes you took after your journey. Ask yourself questions from each perspective. If you can, share your journey with others. Let them give you their interpretations. Listen.

• From the Warrior, who shows up and is ready for action – where did you show up in your journey? What actions did you take?

• From the Teacher, who knows that every story has a lesson and seeks to find it in the journey – where did you notice a lesson in your journey?

• From the Healer, who recognizes that every event has a potential for healing – where did you notice a healing in your journey?

• From the Magician, who translates spiritual insight into practical applications – what is a "real life" application of the insights you received in your journey?

• What are the symbols you noticed in your journey? What universal, cultural, or personal meanings do they have for you?

Aho

Part Three

Continuing Your Journey

Taking Stock

First, let me thank you for your courage and tenacity. It is no mean feat to have journeyed fourteen times. You have come to understand the process, and allowed the learning to illuminate your life. Bravo!

Second, let me thank you for your willingness. By using this book you are becoming more whole, healthy and alive. In living life more fully you become a shining light to others. It is my hope that you will now go out and meet others with whom you are ready to share this process.

At the end of these initial fourteen journeys, it is a good idea to take stock of what you have gained from learning how to journey. In the beginning of this book, I suggested that the journey process can help you answer four important questions:

Who am I?
Where did I come from?
What is important to me?
What is the purpose of my life?

Revisit these questions. Has your journey experience helped you answer them, or changed your answers in some way? Are your answers clearer, deeper, or more far-reaching? I know this is true for me. I hope it is true for you.

Journeying is the beginning of a relationship with divine guidance, which is not always easy to interpret. It takes practice, just like any other worthwhile activity. Divine guidance will often set you upon a path. We all know paths are meant to be walked and followed. Sometimes we are not sure where the path may lead, but from experience we all know that it will go somewhere. A few years ago I asked a friend of mine, "Don't I get a vacation?" He replied that once you set your foot on the path, it's hard to sit down.

In the spirit realm journeys do not end. They only continue.
Aho

Other Journeys

Keep journeying! You are just beginning this exciting process, and many more magical, important journeys await you. Journeying is not something you only do once. It is a process that becomes deeper and more meaningful over time. Accessing the wisdom of your spiritual guides will become a natural part of your life and serve you well until the end of your days on this earth plane.

I am often asked, "Where else can I journey?" or "What should my intentions be?" My answer is always the same: anywhere and anything. The possibilities for journey destinations and intentions are infinite. Literally any person, place, idea, or thing can serve as a framework for a journey. Like everything else in the journey process, this is determined by you – what your challenges are, what your questions are, your needs are, your hopes and dreams are.

Here are some ideas you might consider for other journeys. I must stress that this is a *partial* list. The possibilities for journeys are limited only by your imagination. And as we all know, your imagination isn't limited at all.

It is always a good idea to spend journey time simply getting to know your spirit guide. Go on a few journeys (as many as you'd like) in which your intentions might be stated, "Show me where you live," or "Show me what your life is like," or "Show me what you do all day." Sometimes your guide may change, or you may request a new guide for a new phase of your life, or for a series of journeys. Each time this happens, spend some time with this new guide.

Because this is an intimate relationship that will inform all facets of your life, it is well worth the time to explore your guide's world – their concerns, passions and personality. Let them show you around, and tell you what it is they think you should know.

Another journey idea is to return to a journey. Typically there is much more information available in a journey than we can absorb at once. Many people have ongoing journeys, and will just "drop in" where they left off. Try this if you would like more information about something in a particular journey, or if you want to complete a task that was left hanging, or if you want to talk further with a being you met there.

You may choose to revisit the archetypical places you've already been. The fourteen destinations that we explored in this book are particularly rich sources of information.

Journeying to the East is a good idea when you are starting a new venture of any kind, such as a new job or new relationship. Journeying to the South might be a beneficial if you have a situation developing around passion or a love interest. Journeying to the West might give you information about emotional issues in your life, or if you have something going on that involves water. A friend of mine journeyed to the West when she had some plumbing problems in her house. "Show me what I need to know about my septic tank," was the intention she put forth. (Remember, journeying is a practical tool.) And journeying to the North is often a good idea when you find yourself in need of "deep knowing" or ancestral wisdom.

You can journey to the Upper World to get an "overview" of any situation, and journey to the Lower World to see what lies underneath any of your current issues. Journey to the Warrior when you feel a need for an infusion of courage; journey to the Teacher when you are called upon to be a mentor to someone; journey to the Healer if you or someone you love has a health challenge; or journey to the Magician when you particularly need to see clearly, unhampered by the veils of illusion. Or make any of these journeys for any reason at all.

I have found that journeying to my ancestors is a particularly vivid experience for me. I journey to my Female Ancestor when I am experiencing a major transition. The feminine archetype is concerned with issues such as birth, puberty, marriage, and death, and all the transitions in between. When my children left home, I spent a great deal of time with my Female Ancestor, and again when I went through menopause. I visit my Male Ancestor when I would like information about what my next right action should be in any particular situation. The ancestors are helpful in learning about traditions valued in my culture or my family, and how I might adapt them to my current life. They show me if there's something in the past that can help me, and they show me what past "stuff" I am holding onto that no longer serves me. The ancestors give me information that I need to pass on to my descendants, such as the family stories that hold the wisdom and heart of our lineage. If there are painful stories from the "shadow side," such as secrets of abuse or cruelty, journeying to the ancestors helps heal these old wounds.

Challenges, problems, and opportunities – whatever is going on in your ordinary life – are all reasons for journeying. If you are moving, journey to your new land to discover what you should know in order to be a good earth steward. If you are fighting with your boss, journey to the planet Saturn, which rules authority issues. If you are tending a garden, journey to the broccoli or the roses; ask them what they need. If you are sick or injured, journey to the disease, or to the limb or organ that is hurting. See what they have to say to you. This physical world reflects the spiritual, and vice versa. It is all one, and the more facets we experience, the richer and deeper our lives will be.

Even more ideas for journeys include:

- Gods and goddesses, saints, or gurus from any culture or religion, especially ones for whom you feel kinship.

- The signs of the zodiac, perhaps starting with your sun sign or rising sign.

- Any planet, asteroid, star, or celestial body you are curious about. There is a reason you are drawn there.

- Trees, flowers, fields, or any member of the green growing plant family. I often ask my students to journey to find a plant ally. Just as we have Spirit guides who are often animals, we have allies and helpers in the plant world.

- Rocks, caves, the dirt.

- Rivers, oceans, seas, lakes.

- Winds, hurricanes, tsunamis, storms of any kind.

- Colors. Journey to blue, to red, to magenta, to turquoise, to pink, to eggshell, to chartreuse.…

- Tarot cards or runes that you may have drawn.

- Real, historical, legendary, mythological, or fictional people and places. If you have an affinity for Mozart, journey to Mozart to discover the personal message he has for you. If you love *Gone With the Wind*, journey to Scarlett O'Hara or Tara and ask to be shown what you need to know.

Finally, your intentions do not always need to be specific and focused. You can keep your intention open-ended. "Show me what I need to know right now," is a powerful intention. But be prepared to go to some surprising places!

Eventually you will be able to journey without a drumbeat, or setting sacred space, or any of the rituals we use to ease ourselves into non-ordinary reality. The more we journey, the more connected we are to the spiritual, emotional, and mental information that resides within us. The information you need will come to you easily and powerfully – perhaps when you are doing something mundane, like brushing your teeth. You won't have to take a special journey into non-ordinary reality, because you'll be creating your life *from* non-ordinary reality. The barriers between the worlds will come down. The veils will be permanently thin.

You will have accepted that there are more dimensions present always in your ordinary reality. The journey process allows you to wake up. To use a term from the sixties, it raises your consciousness, which is what evolution is all about.

We are all conduits for Spirit. Journeying keeps our conduits clear so that light can flow through us and illuminate the world.

Aho

Memorable Journeys

Journeys are a powerful transformative tool. Our guides know, understand and want us to thrive. Our best interest is always at the heart of our quest for knowledge and information. These spiritual guides for the journeys lead us to healing and happiness. The following journeys were impactful for my students. May you find them helpful and may you have journeys which impact your life and the lives of those you love.

Healing Grandmother by Shannon

As the drumming begins, I stand at the edge of clear, calm water. My feet in the shallow water, sand squishing between my toes. This is where I begin every journey, I feel at home here, and the anticipation of a new journey fills me with excitement.

I look up, and see my canoe rocking gently in the calm water. The canoe itself is always changing, new details appearing each time I journey. Today there is a pole rising from the back of the canoe, a long piece of cloth knotted around it, fluttering in the breeze. The lantern at the bow, is not lit today. Glistening white oars rest inside, new and untouched.

I step into the canoe, and seat myself on the pile of furs near the back. The furs are soft on my skin, and I wiggle my damp toes deep into the warm fur. I leave the oars alone, and fold my hands in my lap.

I turn to the right, and call to my male ancestors. A weathered old medicine man in full native attire comes forward, beating his drum. Behind him emerges my Grandfather. Recently crossed over, he appears vibrant, young, and tall. He smiles at me. Fish splashes the side of my canoe to announce his presence.
I turn to the left and call my female ancestors. A beautiful woman in long flowing robes stands on the shore. Behind her spirits gather and wait. Deer laps at the water's edge.

In the bow of my canoe I place my guide, Mother Bear. She settles in comfortably, her sheer size should capsize the canoe, but it does not.

For protection, I place my bow and quiver full of arrows behind me. A black crystal appears, glowing with light.

I turn my attention back to Mother Bear, and set my intention for this journey.

"Show me what I need to know about the next step in my path. And please show me healing for my grandmother." (At this time, my grandmother is in the hospital.)

On the next beat of the drum, the glowing light source deep in my chest opened, and a mist of energy and light flow from me. I see my grandmother in front of me, in her hospital room, lying on the bed. The energy flows from me, towards her, and fills her with light. I see her spirit wrapped in a cocoon of light.

I blink, and I am sitting in my canoe. A slight wind ripples the water, and rocks the canoe. I hear the waves lapping at the water's edge. Seagulls scream overhead. The canoe creaks, the fabric tied to the pole snaps and flutters. The smell of salt water and seaweed fill my nose. I feel the spray of seawater on my face as the canoe begins to move.

As the canoe moves, the water changes, and rapids appear in front of me. Fear of capsizing and drowning grips me. My heartbeat quickens as the rapids loom closer, but the oars remain untouched. As the canoe enters the rapids, it strikes the jagged rocks, and begins to break apart. I am tossed clear, and plunged into the churning water.

I open my eyes, I am in deep, dark water, the rapids are gone. There is no light, yet I can see. A gold cord is wrapped around me like a harness. For a while I swim around, gazing at the creatures and plants that come into view. The solitude is calming. Bear paddles past, she too is enjoying her swim. After a while, I feel that it is time to go, so I turn to the golden cord, and follow it as it stretches upward in the darkness.

The cord leads me to the surface, I look up to see it attached to the bow of my canoe. Whole and perfect, my canoe is gently rocking in the breeze, at the center of an expanse of calm water. I climb back into the canoe and the gold cord becomes a necklace around my neck.

I turn to bear, once again in the bow of my canoe, and ask if there is anything else I need to know.

I am shown my Grandfather, he is walking hand in hand with a young woman. They are happy.

A spirit from my left comes forward and she is my Grandmother, my mother's mother. She appears as she did when I was a child, just before she crossed over. I reach out my arms towards her. She opens her arms, and wraps me in a warm embrace. I am filled with love and joy. After a few moments, she whispers to me that it is time to return, and I am back at my journey's start. I step from my canoe into the shallow water, and am home.

I thank my guides and ancestors for their presence and guidance in my journey, and the journey ends with the final beat of the drum.

Impact and Interpretation

I always find it difficult to interpret my own journeys. My critical mind asks if I am just not selecting the meaning I want it to have, rather than the true meaning. However, it is also quite possible that my guides, in their wisdom, have not only shown me the journey, but imparted upon me the ability to understand its meaning.

In this journey the physical health of my grandmother was heavily on my mind, and had been for several days. My guides, with their love and understanding of this, put my mind at ease about her right away. In watching the healing energy pour out of me, and into her, I felt at peace. Now, sometime later, I have come to realize that the connection I have with my grandmother is stronger, and no matter what transpires with her physical body, her spirit is strong and vibrant, and she will never leave me. I believe this is why I saw her spirit wrapped in healing, not just her body.

In the second part of my journey, I am shown rapids and danger ahead. I feel that my guides are showing me that my path may not always seem easy, indeed I often choose the difficult road, but I don't need to be afraid. I ended up in calm, healing water – the element I am most at home with – unhurt, at peace, experiencing a whole new place I would not have found without the rapids. The golden cord says I am protected, I am safe. The canoe being whole a sign that I will survive and be as good as new, or better! I think the return to calm waters also shows that I will not always struggle.

The final part of my journey, in seeing my grandfather happy, and making contact with my other grandmother who has crossed over, is more assurance that I am loved, and protected. It fills me with confidence that I am following the right path.

Aho

Journey to the Elk by Anita L.

I am in a drum making class and we are journeying with the hide of the Elk who has given its life so I can have a drum.

I asked my guide, White Eagle, to show me/explain the spirit of the Elk hide from which I was going to make a drum. This is what I learned:

The Elk medicine of this magnificent animal would guide and protect me with the sureness of its steadiness and awareness. Its protection comes from the Elk's knowingness – senses (smell, sight, hearing) – I could smell and taste the tender sweet grass he was eating in the journey.

I had a sense of calmness in knowing safety – assurance, strength and power of the Elk energy – all will be there reverberating with every beat of this drum.

The Elk was killed – shot and the pain it felt shuddered through me. I felt it and it was nasty. I saw its eyes close in death.

The soul of this Elk lives on in the drum and its energy in the vibration it sends out – keeping the Earth alive and all on it.

I felt so sorry for your death/sacrifice and so grateful for your gift to me. Thank you Elk Spirit; I will use this drum wisely and well.

Aho

Be Wild and Trust by Shiela

In the following journey a student is compelled to explore the feelings brought up from reading the story of my journey.

For several months I travelled to Canada and took care of my ailing Mum; I wrote this journey after returning and reconnecting with many of my students and clients.

The Journey

All my journeys begin imagining myself in a birchbark Spirit canoe; however, for this journey I have a three-masted ship. My Male Ancestor, the Bear, is on my right and my Female Ancestor, my Native American Grandmother, joins us to my left. My Guide for this journey, a Phoenix is in the bow, my Protection, the crystal formation, is behind me in the stern. Then I state my intention. I use all my senses while journeying so not to miss anything. There is a monotonous drumbeat as I journey.

As my journey begins I am standing. On my right Bear is catching Salmon and Grandmother on the left is mending a net. Many guides show themselves in the bow but Phoenix rises and says she will take me where I need to go. The crystal formation is behind me.

Everything is moving very fast, the water, the wind and the ship when I state my intention: Show me how to connect again as I have been absent for a long time.

The crew is scrambling to get into their places – one man has chocolate around his lips. "What?" I ask. "Birthday" they reply. "Whose?" "Tony" and they point to an elderly gent. "Will you dine with me in celebration?" I ask. "All et up" he replies. So I give him a gift – a bell which becomes a light when inverted. "Who will guide me?" Phoenix again says "I will."

Off we go flying like the old sailing ships at an amusement park. I am afraid and say "This is too wild." First, we swerve to the right, then to the middle, then to the left making our way out into the Milky Way. We are heading directly into the middle of the Big Dipper. We wildly make our amusement-park-way up the handle of the dipper. When we are at the end the Big Dipper flips over and I freak: We've tipped the Big Dipper. "Trust" everyone says simultaneously, "you've got to trust that everything will return to exactly as it ought to be."

"What has that got to do with reconnecting?" I ask. "Be wild, have fun, tip things upside down and all will return to the way it is meant to be" is the reply. I thank my guides and return to the place on the river where my journeys begin.

Upon my return to the physical world I notice that Devil's Club is growing at my feet. I was journeying outdoors by a river.

Interpreting the Journey

To understand my journey I use five archetypes. You are the **Visionary**, the one taking the journey. The Enlightened Spiritual **Warrior** decides what action, if any to take in the journeys. The **Teacher** notices the lessons and the **Healer** is aware of the healing in the journey It may be worthwhile to find the healing properties of Devil's Club. The **Magician** brings the insights back into this world and makes them practical, hence Practical Shamanism. By focusing on these five aspects we have a framework for interpreting and using this important information.

In this journey the **Warrior** is willing to be afraid and yet go on the wild ride. The lesson for the **Teacher** appears to be allowing events to unfold easily. The healing of the **Healer** seems to be coming to know that everything is as it should be regardless of appearances. As the **Magician**, I can go to an amusement park, ride the scary rides and notice how I feel. The ability to feel fear and move beyond it is learning to trust so that I can feel at ease and carefree, suspend judgment and open to infinite possibilities. Remember to laugh and be playful. Don't think! Relax. Be discerning about "having to do" and notice when you can just BE.

What do you find relevant for your life in this journey? One of my students found this particular journey to be so emotionally powerful that she has recounted her experience here and how she used this journey as a jumping off point to access the Akashic Records and explore. Here is her description of what happened:

Reading this journey of Shiela's had a profound emotional effect on me. I was moved by the experience of someone having been gone a long time and then returning. Because I didn't know who this was or who I was, I decided to open the Akashic Records for myself and find out.

I ask the Masters, Teachers, and Loved Ones of the Akashic Records: "What do I need to know about my current emotional feelings? What needs healing?"

It seemed I was in seventeenth century France. I was sitting down, working in a field. I was wearing a large white skirt, and I saw it spread out around me. I was extremely sad, as I was missing someone who had been gone a very long time. There was no way to get in touch with this person and no way to know if he/she were still alive.

Then, in my mind's eye, I saw the Six of Wands in the Rider-Waite Tarot deck. It depicts a man on a horse, holding a staff with a Laurel wreath around it, he too has a Laurel wreath upon his head. He has returned home victorious. In the background the townspeople are applauding.

In my Akashic Reading there's a celebration in a large building where many people are gathered around this person. People are dancing, eating and drinking. I watch, separate from the others, not joining in the spirit of the celebration. Although I am relieved this person has returned home, my longing for him/her has been so great that I am unable to feel the joy the others are experiencing.

"How can I heal this lack of feeling now?" I ask. The answer I receive is "Let yourself feel the depth of the emotions in every nook and cranny of your being. Really feel them. Do not avoid them. Continue doing this and things will shift. You will have emotional freedom and be able to enjoy the celebration of life."

I thank the Masters, Teachers, and Loved Ones and close the Akashic Records.

Since this journey, I have allowed myself to cry about the longing I felt in my heart. I have also noticed the changing weather, the birds and ducks at my neighborhood lake, the spring blossoms, the feel of my dog's fur, the taste of delicious food, and the sounds of planes and cars as I sit in my house. All my senses now are heightened.

Aho

Journey for Fear by Brian

The purpose of the Shaman, the teacher has been to show the guides to a path that serves to eliminate suffering in me and in the world. I would like to reflect a journey I did related to questions surrounding Fear within Life. More specifically, the question was how do I proceed as a being of light Indigo child with fear of the past. I was abused as a child and had feelings of guilt, shame and fear of men instilled in me. How do I readily accept strong Yang qualities into life as a healer?

As I called the directions, the Guides of the North pulled me to the element of water. This made a perfect beginning for my travels in the birchbark canoe.

Joining me appeared a Salmon representing female wisdom. She is a King salmon and still saltwater bound. She never speaks and always represents the Yin Power that creates innate knowing. She becomes stern when I doubt myself; she represents survival and knowing. She represents the power to take great journeys, sometimes against currents and streams.

As I called for Male guides, I am joined by a large Bull running alongside my canoe on the shore. His eyes blood red, snorting steam, there is a golden ring in his nose. He represents overt Yang Male energy, the flesh body and raw strength it takes to live among the legged ones. He frightens me yet has never caused harm; he pulls at me when I lack primal strength in my flesh body.

My main guide who is normally a green Boa is replaced by a young boy. He is strong and determined, skimming his hands in the water. He glances back nodding an "OK" that our travel is true. He knows no direction but forward, no service except that which serves him (and me) in this moment. Like a strong young child, he only knows to serve immediate survival.

Traveling as protection, seated in the aft of the canoe is a crystal light. It is like a lantern – creating an aura around all that join my journey, lighting the way for my main guide to see.

We leave the water surface to travel just below, like a submarine just beneath the surface. We become smooth and non-visible to untrained eyes. Joining us from the open sky is Osprey who can see below the water surface and is not afraid to dive. I shape shift to see through his eyes.

I ask my 1000 guides to assist in answering the question of fear. Universally they reflect that I only need to have trust in the direction. That even though my vessel fills with water, I'll never sink; in fact as I travel just beneath the water it is simply ballast that allows me to move undetected. This will make me able to avoid all that will cause me to turn away from this path. Stealth serves so I may serve higher good without visible ego. The Osprey will always be vigilant as he is able to see when I do disappear to travel in the watery wilderness. The Bull reminds me to only use power when necessary and sometimes the appearance of ferocity only acts as a rouse to thwart bad energy or beings when I travel above water. My main guide becomes me as a 4 year old child that at first sign of danger reminds me to fearlessly move ahead in spite of lumps and bumps.

I am reminded that this journey acts to tell and give the answer, that for this time, stealth is not avoidance. I am reminded that to serve visibly without fear of judgment or failure is the goal. The currents will carry, and guides will add strength. Sometimes, I may choose to travel on land and there my guides will never fail me.

The lesson is that Trust and Faith is the antidote to fear.

I return from the journey and into conscious reality knowing the guides have spoken and reinforced the path. I offer thanks to the legged ones, winged ones, swimmers and light beings for joining my travels to seek truth and healing.

Aho

Healing Journey by Anita

The Journey

Sitting in my birchbark canoe, on my right I notice my male ancestors: the trees, some rocks, and a crow. On my left are my female ancestors: my mother, maternal grandmother, and lots of angels. In the bow of my canoe as a guide is my guardian angel. In the back of my canoe as my protection is Archangel Michael.

I set my intention: "Show me what I need to know about healing."

I see myself in the canoe in a lake. All of a sudden, I am in space, orbiting the Earth, and seeing the curvature of the Earth. My angel takes me to a mountaintop. We sit and watch for a while. There is a cabin and a fire inside. She holds me in both places at once. *Allow yourself to be loved*, I hear telepathically. *Allow, allow, allow.* Then she flies me to the lake where we started, and we sit on the lake's shore next to a campfire. We sit there a long time. *Allow, allow, allow*, I hear again, *whatever desire of having, of feeling.* Then we are back in the canoe. The lake turns into a river that opens up to a larger body of water. *Don't worry about what you eat or drink*, I hear. *Just go to the core, which is allow yourself to be loved.* As we emerge into a larger body of water, people who have passed on are reaching their arms toward me. All those people with outstretched arms are a bit overwhelming to me. My guardian angel protects me. I have a knowing that I can trust my experiences and that my angel can be with me always.

Interpreting the Five Archetypes

As the **Visionary**, I see myself experiencing the journey. As the **Warrior**, I show up when I let my angel to hold me and fly me, and when I listen to her guidance. As the **Teacher**, the lesson is to be open and I find myself willing to be loved. It is safe to be loved. As the **Healer**, healing occurs when I desire whatever I want and realize that even then I am safe. As the **Magician**, I can take this experience into the practical world and dream of what I want. I can have my desires. I can be open to other peoples' affection. I can be held and be flown by my angel. In my life I have not been willing to get on an airplane for six years. Now I can, and I'm going to plan a trip!

Aho

An Irish Adventure by Tanya

Intention: Show me in Ireland
Male Ancestors: Wolf, hawk, raccoon, frog
Female Ancestors: Horse, Parrot, Rabbit, Snake
Protection: Giant Tree
Guide: Rabbit Wabbish

The Journey

The canoe shoved off shore and glided off the water to then shift into a dirt road, then the canoe morphed into a wagon, and suddenly we are on old country land bumbling about through a tunnel of trees. We approach a cottage upon some open hills that appeared to be emerald eye candy reflecting Ireland. I jumped out of the wagon ever so light because I had transformed into a fairy. I skipped over to the garden to dance around and play like a child on a playground.

I decided to enter the cottage and I went upstairs out of some instinct inside me. "What did I do here?" I asked out loud. Wabbish told me I painted at this cottage and would go on wild adventures; this is where I stayed when I came to Ireland for artistic inspiration and my sense of freedom.

I jumped out of the large window that looked out on lots of trees and a nearby neighbor's house and landed on a horse. I began riding; I felt so free and giddy, it was wonderful! The horse and I ran far and I soaked up the feeling of the wind around me till we reached a hut at the edge of the forest. I jumped down from the horse and went inside the hut where I took off my fairy skin and hung it up like horse tack and then I pulled down a leprechaun skin and put that on.

I ran off into the forest and located a big giant tree that had a door between two of its roots, and I entered. Inside the tree was a pub. I sat down with a few friends and indulged into a thick stout ale. We danced and sang as the ales kept pouring. After the party left I decided to climb up higher inside the trunk of the tree till I was so high I popped my head out the top of all the tree leaves and caught a big breath of cool air that danced around my nose hair. This feels like déjà vu, like the scene from *The Hobbit* where Bilbo sticks his head out of the trees in Mirkwood.

A dragon came out of nowhere and scooped me up out of the top of the tree and we took a short ride to the edge of the sky on top of a grand hill. We sat quietly staring off as the reds and oranges of the sunset mixed against the emerald greens of the vast hills. I realized this moment right here right now was my pot of gold.

Then the canoe transported us back to the starting shores, and as I climbed out of the canoe I gave thanks to all who were involved and it ended.

Interpreting the Journey

I have always deeply felt a connection to a location I have never been, at least not in this lifetime. My intention in this journey was to make something that has often times felt unobtainable and show myself it's closer than I think. The shedding of skins sticks out as profound because it represents removing part of yourself to change into something else. I get that I will either be doing some huge changing or will reinvent myself to get to a great goal I am looking to achieve. Perhaps this journey has helped shed off a layer of doubt thus making it easier for me to make a trip to Ireland happen. When I asked out loud, "What did I do here?" some remembering of another life is popping up or my soul is dropping some hints on connections to my goal of going to Ireland. My guide told me I painted in the cottage in that room and I feel this shows a piece of my soul work is lingering in Ireland for me to find and collect. The pub scene where I was drinking and dancing with friends and at the end where I say, "my pot of gold is in the experience," both show that this journey is giving me great meaning in having a chance to go to Ireland. The longing and wanting turns into a need because I have things that have to be accomplished.

A few days after this journey opportunity presented itself; I got in touch with a friend who has been wanting to go to Ireland as well and got her on board with me. I bought my plane ticket and my friend and I planned the whole trip out and booked a hotel and transportation. I was amazed on how natural, fast and aligned everything was for me to make this trip happen. Once I decided this trip was absolutely going to happen and nothing was going to stop it because I knew it was my destiny, the energies all shifted and it unrolled with great ease and excitement.

Aho

Giving Like Before by Shiela

The Journey

Lightning bolts flash from my palms as Bear, my Male Ancestor shows up in a waistcoat. Grandmother Elder, my Female Ancestor is crocheting and says, "Go on without me." Hawk, my guide sits in the bow and behind is my protection a crystal formation. The intention is: "Show me what I need to know about forgiveness."

Looking down we notice there is a rectangular hole in the canoe, so we beach it. Turning right we walk towards a channel leading to a small island. The island is familiar as we often go to gaze into a well located there. An image appears of a single mast felucca, a small boat in which the offerings are sent out to float on the Ganges. Turning away from the well we set free some of our own prayer baskets. They seem to be coming back to us. Hawk pulls on a string attached to the baskets and pulls them out into the stream where he removes the strings – No strings attached!

Traveling along our path there are many sites where we offer forgiveness in the form of baskets set adrift. What is most poignant is that I am the first one to be forgiven – this is a moving and humbling experience as I was "thinking" that we were going to forgive others!

From his perch on a tree branch my Chinese medicine guide Li Win offers me advise on a remedy I can use and then says, "Go higher." Climbing up to the tops of the trees I see further into the woods. With this new perspective I notice smoke rising. "Jump up and walk on the tree tops," says Li Win, so I do. At the smoldering fire I rekindle the flames. From out of nowhere a skeleton appears and pulls me behind a big tree just before a herd of the smallest demons I have ever seen surges forward and stamps out the fire. Yelling and screaming they dash back into the forest.

The skeleton leads me to a meadow where I understand the message: Forgiveness is like grass; it is always growing. The meadow is filled with beautiful colorful flowers and I am told they are like regrets and I should enjoy them with no remorse. These flowers are here to be picked and brought inside. We gather a fragrant bouquet.

The journey ends in gratitude.

Interpreting the Journey

The **Visionary** is me as I am having the journey. As the **Warrior** I beach the canoe which has a hole in it. Sometimes being down to earth is what's required. As the **Teacher** the lesson is that by crossing the channel we arrive at a place of wisdom. Do not be afraid of taking a new or different path. We are all one so forgive yourself first – what a powerful lesson. As the **Healer** the healing is that the guide, Hawk, detaches the string and reminds us to not hold on to regrets. The regret is really what motivates us to forgive. We are missing something – the friendship or the experience. So it is the missing or our regret that pulls us to the act of forgiving. As the **Magician** – Place your regrets in a fragrant floral basket with no strings attached and LET FORGIVENESS FLOW. What regrets are you still holding on to? Who (starting with yourself first) have you not forgiven? The word forgive really means to give like before. To whom and for what are you no longer giving like before? Yes, like before the event. Where have you stopped the energy flow?

Aho

Anita's Shamanic Journey Poem

I step into my spirit canoe
Guides and protection surround me
On a journey I'm ready to go
Wherever they wish to take me

In my hand is my pink crystal heart
I don't know how it got there
I look down at what I'm wearing
Jeans, boots and bright blue hair

I look up and the canoe is moving
I look out beyond the horizon
As dusk shows pink, orange and blue
Stars appear and are rising

With my blanket on and my hoodie up
And my legs stretched out in front of me
My guide leads the way to another world
While I wonder what I will see

Under the water we dive so deep
It happens all of a sudden
Magical creatures do I meet
In corals and seaweed and dens

Out of the water we shoot in the air
With sun and sky all around us
We fly over trees and mountains and fields
The earth's beauty surrounds us

Out of the canoe and into the forest
A unicorn is there to greet me
It rides me through the trees
Where more creatures meet me

Fairies and monkeys and zebras and elves
Curious as they approach me
Go on their way and continue to play
And deeper into their land I see

All of a sudden I'm alone and scared
Even the unicorn has left me
My heart is pounding, my body shaking
It's dark and I cannot see

What do I do? Where do I go?
Someone help me please
Be still and do nothing I hear a voice say
Relax and sit and breathe

I sit for a time then see a soft glow
The darkness is lifting and lightening
Come with me into the tree
A bright being comes in sight of me

She takes my hand, an angel she is
And leads me to the trunk of a tree
She opens its door and takes me inside
And puts angel essence around me

Now warm and secure with angel protection
I shift my shape to a utility pole
And straighten up tall as the tree is high
Spin around and plunge into a hole

Under the earth I go down and down
Into the rocks, the roots and the ground
Shivering cold when I finally stop
I go back to my shape and look around

I warm as I walk through the hard packed earth
Freely I move through soil and sand
Water and tunnels and bugs and more
Branches and brambles and my own hands

Let me out, I'm ready to come up
Panic hits me for a time
Stop and breathe the angel speaks
And I know I will be fine

Just then the bedrock gives way
And opens up into a cave
I walk out to the sea and step on the beach
Then I'm fully consumed by a wave

Up from the water I spot my canoe
An eagle comes by to fly me
I hop on its back and up I go
And back in my boat I feel free

Back where I started
On top of the bay
Thank you guides and helpers
Thank you for showing me the way

Aho

Appreciation, a Journey to Love by Shiela

The Journey

My journeys begin by imagining a birchbark Spirit canoe. My Male Ancestor, the Bear, is on my right and my Female Ancestor, my Native American Grandmother, joins us to my left. My Guide for this journey, a Peacock, is in the bow with my Protection, the crystal formation, behind me in the stern. Then I state my intention. I use all my senses while journeying so not to miss anything. There is a monotonous drumbeat as I journey.

In this journey I am doing the typical busy human thing, I am multitasking, teaching a journey class and journeying for you. We are very proud of this ability, multitasking; perhaps we can learn from the animals how to be fully present.

In this journey my Bear seems happy, dancing his way to me, Grandmother on the left is crocheting, Peacock has brought his mate a dazzling white Peahen with him and my Crystals are in the rear.

I state my intention "Show me what I need to know about Love." The Peacock and Peahen gaze into each others' eyes and their heads form a heart. Corney! I think. They continue. She says "He is clearly more colorful than I but he takes the heat for me when our babies are small." He says "You have more choices than I – what with your pure color and focus on the small ones." Back and forth they go listing the attributes that each values in the other. Many long hours go by and they are glowing with admiration. You do this and you do that….

"So, this is Love?" I ask. "There's more" they say "but for now this is enough." The journey ends and I give thanks for the ancestors, protection and my guides who teach about Love.

Interpreting the Journey

In this journey the **Warrior** listens and asks for more but it is not to come. The lesson for the **Teacher** appears to be watching the mutual respect of the Pea couple, and the healing for the **Healer** seems to be in the dancing Bear and crocheting Grandmother each doing their own thing independent but in tandem. As the **Magician,** bringing wisdom into the practical world, I can dance and take up a hobby like knitting or crocheting as I wait for more. The winter is a perfect time of year for those activities as we await the return of the light. The pure white Peahen reminds me of Imbolc on February 2 when the light changes. Pay attention to the day coined by the western world as Groundhog Day. Watch how the light changes after that day and we come once again into the rebirthing of the spring just six weeks away. Plan for the spring of your life, be open to a beloved. You can even watch the movie *Groundhog Day*; it has many shamanic lessons.

Aho

Your Journey Practice

You might wonder, now that you have finished these initial journeys, what your journey practice should look like. How often should you journey? Should you journey in the morning or the evening, or once a week, once a day, or once a month? Should you do journeys regularly, or only when you encounter a situation that needs clarification?

There are no right answers to these questions. Your journey practice should serve *your* needs. Some people journey three or four times a day, every day, for every reason. Once you have learned what a great tool you have at your disposal, it is natural to want to use it, especially in the beginning. When I was new to the journey practice, I spent nearly as much time in the otherworld as I did in this one! This is a fine way to make journeying an integral part of your life.

But it is equally fine to journey once a year, if that is what serves you best. You must experiment with journeying to discover the correct process for you. If you have a demanding job, children, a spouse, volunteer activities, and an active social life, adding another "must" or "should" to your life probably won't serve you very well. You are on your journey, not someone else's.

I know people whose journey practice consists only of a week-long journey retreat once or twice a year, in which they spend most of their waking hours journeying, gathering guidance for the upcoming months. Others journey in the bathtub every evening after the children are asleep. Some people journey every morning, helping them to set their intention for the day ahead, and others journey at night, to ask Spirit's help in discerning the meaning of that day's events, or to ask for powerful dreams. Some people even journey on their commuter train on the way home from work.

It doesn't matter when, where or how often you journey. What does matter is that you use this powerful tool. It will help you pay attention to your life.

Your life is happening now. Be there for it.

Aho

Journeying With Others

To deepen your journey experience immeasurably, journey often with other people. Be willing to share your journeys and listen to their feedback; the insights that your journeys give them become your own. Be open to hearing what their journeys have to teach you as well. Share this knowledge and you may be able to help others profoundly. In this way you will gain the full depth and richness of shamanic journeying, for as we have seen, others' journeys are your journeys, and vice versa. Journeying together will bring you healing and wisdom beyond time and space.

Although there is no right or wrong way to journey with others, there are frameworks and processes that work well for journey groups. Start by gathering a group of people together in any room that has sufficient space for everyone to lie down or recline comfortably without touching each other. Ideally the room should not be too noisy; although complete silence is not necessary, distractions such as televisions or radios should be kept at a minimum.

The size of your group does not matter. It can be as few as two, or as many as the room will hold. The ideal number of journeyers is five, to match the number of archetypes you will be interpreting from, but this is certainly not mandatory. Your journey group may be made up of friends or strangers. Encourage people to bring others unknown to the rest of the group. Each person will bring his or her unique perspective and valuable wisdom to the journey process. It is also not necessary to have a designated facilitator or leader, but it may be helpful to give one person the responsibility for turning on and off the mp3. Then just follow the directions in this book, listening to the Sacred Drumming mp3, *Practical Shamanism*, available on www.shielabaker.com.

After your group has finished journeying, take five to ten minutes for everyone to write down a few notes about their journeys. Then come back together as a group. You may sit in a circle on the floor, or around a table, or any configuration that appeals to you.

Experiment with different seating arrangements to see what works best.

The first visionary then relates their journey while the others listen. While listening, do not offer judgments or comments. Just listen. After the journey has been told, the person on the visionary's right speaks from the Warrior perspective. They will tell where they saw the person show up. Then the next person to the right speaks from the Teacher perspective, telling where they heard a lesson. Continuing around the circle, the next person listens and speaks from the Healer perspective, giving their opinion on where they saw a healing in the visionary's journey. Finally, the last person speaks from the Magician perspective, telling what possible actions they think are suggested by the journey. With this process, the journeyer will be gifted with four different perspectives of his or her journey, from four different sources.

The power and value of these gifts is truly astonishing. Not only is the journeyer blessed with a richer and deeper knowledge, the listeners are given a profound teaching and healing in learning to trust themselves. When you are the listener, don't worry if you feel blank, or cannot see a lesson, healing, or whatever. There is no pressure to be profound. In fact, usually the first thing that comes into your head is the best thing to say. It is uncanny how often the remark that you think is "stupid," is exactly what the other person needs to hear.

Continue in this way until all members of your group have had a chance to be the visionary and share their journeys. If you always start with the warrior on the visionary's right, everyone will also get an opportunity to listen and speak from the different archetypes. This develops your ability to listen effectively from many different viewpoints.

After you have journeyed together for a while, you might begin to notice some similarities and synchronicities in your journeys. This is a common occurrence, and signifies our interconnectedness. Many times an element will show up in more than one journey for more than one person. Pay attention when this happens! For instance, if three people in your journey group report seeing a white mountain, that mountain has significance not only for those people, but for the group as a whole, and the community you live in. The white mountain is not there by accident. Spirit is speaking to you. It is up to you to explore the meaning of the white mountain to your group. What action is being suggested?

After you have completed sharing and interpreting your journeys, remember to close the circle, and thank Spirit for the wisdom you have gained.

Journey together often. You may want to gather once a week, or once a month, for a set number of weeks or months. Or you might want to keep your gatherings looser and more informal, coming together simply when it feels right. Remember, there is no right way to journey. And since there's no right way, it follows that there is no wrong way. You simply cannot do this wrong.

Aho

Journey Creations

Non-ordinary reality is not only the source of information and wisdom from Spirit, it is also the source for artistic creativity. A wonderful way to concretize your journeys into your life on this plane is to use them as the raw material for art. New ideas for poems, stories, paintings, sculpture, songs, symphonies, recipes, buildings, and so on have been birthed within journeys.

This is another reason to record your journeys in a notebook, or an audio recorder, or somewhere. They become a vast storehouse of creative energy.

One of my favorite arts, accessible to everyone, is the art of collage. It is well suited for making the journey experience real. You can make a collage for each journey, or series of journeys. For collage material, you can use images out of magazines or greeting cards; photographs; ordinary objects from around your house like string or bottle caps; natural wonders such as leaves or flowers, beads or bones; snippets from old letters; cloth, ribbons or lace; your own drawings and paintings; or anything else that represents or symbolizes the objects, beings and meanings in your journey. Glue them on a board or canvas or wall, in whatever configuration pleases you.

Besides collage, you can make your own drum, or rattles, or medicine bag, or other ceremonial objects that bring your journeys into this reality. One of my students painted her drum with colorful portraits of each being she encountered on her journeys over the years. The drum took years to complete, but now she has a vivid pictorial record of her non-ordinary reality. Some of my students have made embroidered "medicine bags"; sewing a leather or cloth pouch and embroidering their own designs upon it, and then filling it with small objects which remind them of their journeys.

It does not matter what kind of art you make from your journeys. It doesn't even matter if that art is *good* as defined by the artistic rules of our society. It only matters that you use these gifts of Spirit to create *something*. Creativity is your birthright. It comes with being alive.

Aho

Akashic Records

Everyone consciously or unconsciously wants to know that there's a pathway through life. Often we seek something or someone to hold your hand as we go through life's challenges. This book is intended to be your hand holder so that you can discover and have the experience of trusted and known spirit guides and understand that you are held.

I was thinking about the Akashic Records, and I was thinking about how when I first heard about the Akashic Records I was saying "Well, so what?" How could this be useful? I have the oldest thing, shamanism, I have my guides so how is it that anything could be more useful than that?

A few years went by and I was suffering. And I use that word on purpose. I was suffering with joint discomfort, I had been advised that I needed a hip replacement. I was in such a desperate state that I asked for an Akashic reading. In that reading, what happened was I was told that within six weeks – in the Akashic Records they don't often talk about time – but I was told that within six weeks everything could be taken care of and I would be out of pain. They told me to stop being prideful and ask for help! That impressed me and it also brought up my skepticism. I thought that as a spiritual teacher I ought to be able to heal myself and I refused to consider that surgery might be the best alternative I knew at the time.

The next week I called to see about getting an appointment. I got an appointment right away. While I was on the phone, feeling skeptical, I tested out my skepticism and said, "Well *if* I need surgery, how long until I could have that?" She excused herself for a moment, when she came back she responded that within a month that I could have the surgery. So that fit within the six weeks; I went to see the doctor and he told me that absolutely I needed the surgery and that I could not do the healing on my own.

That kind of made me annoyed because being a spiritual person and a spiritual teacher and a spiritual healer, I thought that I ought to be able to heal myself. So, I had an Ah Ha! moment. In my understanding the soul carries our body, and the body sometimes can't heal itself, so we need something or someone outside of ourselves. When I went to the surgeon and he said that I needed surgery and got the date within the time frame suggested in the Akashic Records, it became really apparent to me that I was missing something. By allowing my skepticism to disregard the powerful tool of accessing the Akashic Records for help and healing I was denying myself and others.

Thus I began to have a little more respect for the Akashic Records – well a lot more respect for the Akashic Records. I was told in that reading that within six weeks I would be pain free, which did indeed happen and I was told that I could open the Akashic Records for others, which indeed is happening. I began to open the Akashic Records for myself and soon I began to open the Records for others; now it is one of my healing services.

I think that sometimes our human ignorance and arrogance doesn't allow us to be open enough for the gifts that are being given to us. My lesson in this was that I thought I had the ultimate healing tool, in shamanism and its many gifts of spirit guides and shamanic healings. I learned by being willing and open to explore the information that I was given that within six weeks what had taken a toll on my physical, emotional and spiritual life for years could be shifted. I used my new belief in and connection to the Akashic Records to explore the possibility of relief from trauma.

Inadvertently, I discovered that people could and did get healings while we were in the Records on their behalf. I had been opening the Records for a couple years when clients told me about their experiences. Often I didn't know that they needed a physical healing because in the session they would be talking about other things. When they would reflect back to me a few weeks after the session they would say, "Oh, well you know, I had this little spot; I had an MRI or I had a CAT scan or I had an X-Ray, and there was a little spot, and when I went back for the next exam, that little spot was gone." And they would remember that in the Akashic Records a healing had happened.

So I began to play with the idea that in the Akashic Records, because it holds all future possibilities, it holds the possibility of healing. And it doesn't have anything to do with Shiela the personality. It has to do with opening that conduit and then sitting in the presence of the beings that come, your Masters, Teachers and Loved Ones, for you to receive what's available there.

Since that time the Akashic Records are opened, the information that's being asked for happens and a healing can occur. Oftentimes I am told "You go ahead and go on with what you're doing here, but we're going to go over here and do a healing on this person." Sometimes soul parts come home. I've had that happen a number of times that a soul part will be brought forward and introduced to the person in the Akashic Records session.

For someone who's never heard of the Akashic Records what is a simple way to explain it?

The Akashic Records are every thought, deed, action, intention that the soul has from its inception to the present moment and all future possibilities. Because it's not so much the acts that the person/personality does as the intention behind the acts. Sometimes we mess up. We don't intentionally mean to mess up, we are human. So it's the intention that we're holding, which is one of the things I really love about the Akashic Records. We now know from our spiritual teachings that intention is what's really important. The Akashic Records help us understand that affirmation of our soul's intention. So that's a really clear, concise definition of what the Akashic Records offer us.

Quantum physics has apparently discovered that there's a place somewhere that the Akashic Records are held. What I've noticed is that every person who has been in classes with me opening the Akashic Records has a different experience of what the Records are. While it sounds like it ought to be exactly the same for everyone, it appears that we have an individual destination, if you will, about how we see the Akashic Records. So everyone has an individual experience, although the primary thing is that they are all in the Akashic Records as it appears to them. So, it's a little bit like bacon. If you happen to like bacon and you happen to like it crispy, that's your way of liking it. Now somebody else might like it crispy on the edges but soft and pliable in the middle. There doesn't appear through anything that I've been experiencing that there is a firm commonality about how the Records are or where exactly they are or what they look like. Just like dogs, there are dozens of different kinds of dogs. Not everyone is attracted to the same kind of dog, but the overriding thing about us on this planet is that we seem to have a different perspective on similar things.

Who has access to the Akashic Records? I think a better question is, Who doesn't? There's a saying that any motivated person can … whatever. You lose weight, train up their body or learn to do something. I believe the same thing is true of the Akashic Records, that any motivated person can open the Akashic Records. Like the intentions for being in the Akashic Records, the same thing is true. You intend to get information, then you can have access. And right now, Linda Howe, who has written several books on the Akashic Records, has done this wonderful thing where she has brought to us a prayer for opening the Akashic Records.

But I believe that there are other ways to open them as well. And I might not be familiar with them, but readers of this book might have found and might be finding ways to open the Akashic Records. You might even do it in a shamanic journey. So, bottom line, any motivated person has access, and not everyone will want to do it for themselves or for anyone else. I have this idea that everyone can heal themselves and probably everyone could heal someone else. It's a desire, first of all. And then out of that desire comes a determination to figure out how. Kind of like cooking. You have to have a desire to cook something. Then you're going to discover the recipe and how to do it. And you're going to *play* with the recipe. And maybe it's a little too salty for you, so you leave some of the salt out, but geez, you'd like cranberries in there, so you put some cranberries in. It's a little bit like that.

I think one of the reasons that I'm speaking to this in a book, *Journeys of Transformation*, is that there are multiple ways to transform and that the Akashic Records appears at this moment to be one of the most ancient ways, even pre-dating shamanism. I'm imagining our souls probably pre-date our ability to communicate with words. Probably the Akashic Records pre-date us even wanting to know and pass on our history or pass on our stories. So it's possible and probable that the Akashic Records pre-date our human knowledge base. And it might even be, which I think would be kind of an interesting thing to discover, is what were we? What was our soul prior to being our soul right now in this incarnation? That sounds like an interesting thing to ask about.

Now we've discovered the next piece. Who was I before I was this, this personality? One of my colleagues told me that I was a bear in another incarnation and that rings true because I have a Bear as my Male Ancestor. And my Male Ancestor for decades has been Bear. So I wasn't surprised by that, but I *was* surprised by that. On a conscious level it didn't occur to me that, oh, my Male Ancestor is showing up as a bear because I used to be a bear. So, some of the questions that we might not be knowing to ask about the Akashic Records, as you're reading this, they might bubble up for you.

When you access the Akashic Records to whom are you speaking? Oh, that's a beautiful question. We are connecting with the Masters, Teachers, and Loved Ones. It appears that the Loved Ones are people that you've known in this lifetime who have crossed over, by that I mean they are dead, and so it could be grandparents, great grandparents, aunts and uncles, even your own parents who have left this physical plane. And the Masters and Teachers, our Masters, I kind of think of them as like your guides who have been with your soul for eternity.

Whereas our Teachers or guides have mastery over things, I don't think about them in the same way that I think about Masters. Our Masters are our mentors throughout all of our incarnations. In a journey many, many years ago, I met a Chinese master who was with me for a number of months and gave me information that was necessary at the time. So it might be that he was one of my Masters in another incarnation – one of my soul's masters. And then the Teachers can be physical world teachers that we've had when we're here, they can be teachers from another time, another dimension.

The most helpful kinds of questions are: what, why, where, and how. How can I move forward in my life in the area of love, for example? You may get some very interesting answers of what to release in your life and what to draw in. These are often practical and useful things to do in the practical world, like go to a particular event or place. This kind of real life advice is helpful and will open many avenues of pleasure and fun. As well deep healing can occur.

Aho

Bust Your Bogus Beliefs

We live our lives out of beliefs that are generational. If you look at your grandparents, they are not and did not and will not live the same kind of life that you are living. Look at what you want in life, your hopes dreams and aspirations. These are your unfulfilled desires, what you "appear" to not have. Write down any desire. If you want a house and don't have one look at all the beliefs around not having this house such as: I'm too old/young to have a house, houses cost too much, I am a woman and I will never make enough money to buy a house I want – all of those things that are holding you back from having a house, actually write those down as your beliefs about this.

Things will come up that you had no idea were even part of the buying a house. As you begin to reflect on the things that you've written down. You know, I'm a woman. I can't get up on the roof and repair my roof if that needs happening, then you get to look at where did that belief came from? And not only do you get to look at where did this limitation come from, but is that what you actually believe now? Then, with that information, armed with that information, you can go, well, where did it come from? And you can ferret around in your past, in your present, in your future and figure out where it came from. And then you can ask this question, which is I think the biggest part. Is this my belief or one that was given to me?

We are one of the first generations *en masse* to question our beliefs. Before, we just did what we were told to. The rebellious adolescent spiritual part of us says, well is that true for me? Because more people are discovering their truth and walking their talk. So then we look at whether it's true for us and we find out that yes, some things are our truth. You know, like yes, I am a woman and I don't want to go up on my roof, so I'm good with that. Thank you, Aunt Sally, who with all good intention gave me that belief. Then we can go, oh, okay, I'm good with that belief. Yes that is one of my beliefs.

Or no, you know, I'm not good with that belief. That belief doesn't make any sense to me any longer. And we can source it, which means take it back to where we got it from. In our imagination, and sometimes in the physical world, we can get out a little box, write that belief down, put that little unwanted belief in the box, wrap it all up, seal it all up with Scotch tape, put on a nice beautiful bow, and then energetically or in the physical world, give it back to that person. That concretizes that we have energetically let go. What even works better is to actually cut the cord. We are all corded to our beliefs and where they come from. While I'm doing that cord cutting, I'm using my index finger and middle finger and I'm making little scissor motions. So we cut the cord to that belief which is now a beautiful package and send it back to the person, place or thing that gave it to us, which frees us up to have a different belief. It is not that you need to replace all those beliefs with something else, because clearing them out is oftentimes enough. It's like clearing the clutter. You don't need to go get some more clutter. So if you need a new belief, by all means, get a new belief, but if you don't need a new belief, then just let that be cleared out of the way.

Armed with all of that, armed with looking at what I want and the beliefs that are stopping me, holding me back from having it, looking at who they came from – sourcing them – and then returning them, clears up a lot of energy. And the way that most people hold energy is in their body. So you might even notice that on a physical level, you start to thin down or add to. Because all of us have something going on in the realm of our body. Finding somebody who is one hundred percent happy with their body is really rare. So you might notice that the energetic releasing may also release from your body through detoxing. And some things may come to you. So this affects not just your psyche and not just your emotions. When you free things up, when you clear them out, emotionally let go of them, then what happens is there's a sense of freedom that you didn't have before. So it's beneficial for the mind, the body, and the spirit.

Why is it important to bust your bogus beliefs or to move past those things? Let's use the image of climbing a hill. If you come to a creek and you stop at the creek – and creeks have water and water is emotions, so there's a metaphor in that that I'm using right here – so you come up to the creek and you go, well, I can't cross that creek. So you stay there. And then you have a barrier. Some people sit there for a while until they get the courage, the heart. The word courage comes from the word *coeur*, which is French, means heart. So having cour-age is having the heart to go on. Then you can come to a place where you go, oh, do I need a tool to cross this little creek? And maybe you notice that there's a fallen tree, so it's not too big, so you drag it over and then you can walk across that. Sometimes you can look in the water and go, oh it's not too deep. You can take off your shoes and walk across. Sometimes it's not too wide and you can leap across. But oftentimes in your life those barriers, those things that stop you are your beliefs. Once you use a tool, figure out a way to get across the creek then you can have an experience moving beyond your beliefs. You have moved beyond a barrier that was a gift (the belief from someone else) and found your way through.

We're not here to be limited. We're here to have access to the infinite possibilities of our lives. And look at all the people who are now waking up. Look at all the people who are waking up in what used to be called the elder years. All those folks who are in their sixties right now needing to go back to work, they are reinventing themselves. This whole process of looking at your beliefs is a reinvention and it's a stripping away of the limitations. When we're limitless, there's no stopping us. There's achieving many more goals, and the more of us who do this, then the more of us who *can* do this. We become models for others. And some of it's totally inadvertent. Nobody necessarily sets out to be an explorer, but we begin to explore and we begin to share those explorations, because when someone changes something, their energy shifts. When their energy shifts, sometimes there's a glow about them, and people start to look at you: Oh, did you get your hair done? Did you lose weight? They won't know what it is, but they'll begin to ask, they get curious and they want what you are having! Then more of us who ask and get curious, the more those folks who have made these shifts can pay it forward and give us a hand up as opposed to giving idle untested advice.

Then we begin to walk the path together. And I believe that's part of what we're here to do is to walk those paths together, so we're not just isolated all by ourselves. Which brings us back to this interconnectedness, the interconnectedness of all beings. Well, praise the Internet for having gotten that out there. And we're starting to learn that people who we feared at some time, there's no fear anymore because we're understanding that they're human just like us, and they have human desires.

What are human desires? We all want to be lovable, capable and worthwhile. Those are very common goals. What are our three foibles? I'm not lovable, I'm not capable, and I'm not worthwhile. What we know from offering inspirational messages and pictures of ourselves on our website or Facebook is that somebody finds us lovable, capable and worthwhile. They like what we have to say. They want to be our friends. And when you start to do that, you notice that there are other people who want to hang out with you, they want to be in your energy field. Then, inadvertently, or hopefully consciously by this point, you become a guide. When you popped out into the world, when you were born, you didn't necessarily know you were going to do that. But it's part of growth, it's part of evolving, and it's part of giving back. That's ultimately what we're here to do is walk our talk and give back to the world. Leave it a better place than when we found it.

Aho

Available Guidance

Shiela Baker offers healing and personal development through Shamanic classes, workshops, retreats, Vision Quests, seasonal ceremonies and celebrations. *Practical Shamanism* mp3 is available at www.shielabaker.com

These offerings are a way for you to connect with others who are following this path, all the while learning and replenishing your spirit.

Personally, I am available for soul retrieval and after-care, individual counseling, Shamanic Tarot, accessing the Akashic Records and shamanic journey consultations. To find out more about my offerings, please visit my website at www.shielabaker.com

My deepest heartfelt wish for you is that you remember who you are, where you came from, and discover your passionate purpose. Then live it!

Aho

Suggested Readings

Archive for Research in Archetypal Symbolism, *The Book of Symbols: Reflections on Archetypal Images*, Taschen, 2010.

Ted Andrews, *Animal Speak: The Spiritual and Magical Powers of Creatures Great and Small*, Llewellyn Publications, 1993.

Angeles Arrien, *The Four-Fold Way: Walking the Paths of the Warrior, Teacher, Healer and Visionary*, Harper San Francisco, 1993.

Melanie Barnum, *The Book of Psychic Symbols*, Llewellyn Publications, 2012.

Joan Borysenko, *Fire in the Soul: A New Psychology of Spiritual Optimism*, Warner Books, 1994.

Deepak Chopra, *The Spontaneous Fulfillment of Desire: Harnessing the Infinite Power of Coincidence*, Harmony Publishing, 2003.

J. C. Cooper, *An Illustrated Encyclopaedia of Traditional Symbols,* Thames & Hudson, 1987.

Tom Cowan, *Shamanism as a Spiritual Practice for Daily Life*, Genealogical Services/Crossing Press, 1996.

Brooke Medicine Eagle, *The Last Ghost Dance: A Guide for Earth Mages*, Wellspring/Ballantine, 2000.

Michael Harner, *The Way of the Shaman*, Harper San Francisco, 1990.

Linda Howe, *How to Read the Akashic Records: Accessing the Archive of the Soul and Its Journey*, Sounds True, 2010.
Sandra Ingerman, *Soul Retrieval: Mending the Fragmented Self Through Shamanic Practice*, Harper San Francisco, 1991.

Carl Jung, *Man and His Symbols*, Dell, 1968.

John Mathews, *The Celtic Shaman: A Handbook*, Element Books, 1991.

Don Miguel Ruiz, *The Four Agreements: A Practical Guide to Personal Freedom*, Amber-Allen Publishing, 1997.

Don Miguel Ruiz, *The Mastery of Love: A Toltec Wisdom Book*, Amber-Allen Publishing, 1999.

Nicki Scully and Angele Werneke, *Power Animal Meditations: Shamanic Journeys with your Spirit Allies*, Bear & Co., 2001.

Hank Wesselman, *Spirit Medicine: Healing in the Sacred Realms*, Hay House, 2004.

About the Author

Shiela Baker, a practicing & teaching Shaman, is a Mental Health Therapist, a trained Registered Nurse, a Children's Mental Health Specialist and holds a Master's Degree in Dance Movement Therapy. She uses many tools to help the soul's evolution including Shamanic Tarot, the Akashic Records, Soul Retrieval with After-Care, Shamanic Counseling & home & business blessings.

As a child, Shiela had experiences of grownups asking for her opinion and then offering guidance beyond her youthful knowledge. She watched as the recipients used or did not use the information. Her keen observation led her to understand that information is not enough. Implementation seemed then and now to be important in her life and the lives of others who seek help. With this awareness and the ability to listen deeply she trusts that there is divine wisdom which when used in everyday life leads to a life well lived, divinely guided and bliss filled. It is with this desire that all beings are healthy, whole and happy that her teachings are powerfully uplifting.

She believes that we are on Earth School to heal our wounds, find our passion, and live an abundant prosperous life. Then from this empowered place, we may help one another to be magnificent and bring our unique gifts into being. You are the only one in the Universe who has your special gift and without your gift we are all missing the healing and joy you may offer.

Shiela uses alternative thinking for practical solutions. When one combines compassion, humor and insight with Spiritual principles, healing and empowered growth occurs. You can have the life of your dreams!

Shiela loves to travel and spends time in her home near Seattle, Washington, and her native Canada.

More information about Shiela and her spiritual services may be found on her website: www.shielabaker.com She welcomes your inquiries and comments either through the web site, via phone at 206-903-9404 or email at shiela@shamanweaver.com

Shiela's heartfelt desire is that you journey often and share your wisdom with your friends and family.

Aho

23943884R00148

Made in the USA
San Bernardino, CA
05 September 2015